Best RV Tips
From RVTipOfTheDay.com

These tips come from fellow RVers... weekenders to full-timers of many years... who have "been there, done that." and happily share their experiences so you don't have to learn the hard way.

Edited by

Steven Fletcher & Fran Crawford

Fletcher Publications

About The Editors

It didn't take long after acquiring our first Recreational Vehicle (RV) that we realized we were destined to be 'full timers'. The was in the early 1990s. Before that acquisition we had tent camped and even ventured across the country from northern California to western Pennsylvania and back through Washington and Oregon in Steven's boxy old 1965 Chevy van. Those were the days, my friends.

Steven had joined an online email group that became RVclub.com* which became known to its members as the Virtual Campfire. With thousands of members all connected through email the knowledge base was huge. Ask just about any RV question and you were sure to get several good answers.

Whenever two or more of these email-corresponding folks would end up nearby each other they would have a 'get-to-gether' (GTG). What fun to get a group together, put faces with names/email addresses. We miss those days but we are still in contact with the friends we made back then.

We also enjoy our membership in the Escapees Club with it's Escapades (rallies) and Birds of a Feather (BOFs) groups. The BOF we joined was for woodcarvers and have attended many annual gatherings.

As the internet was developing, Steven built the website RVbasics.com as a place to archive all the information he learned about RVing. The website has it's own email group and just like the RVClub members, they helped each other with solutions to problems they encountered in the RV lifestyle. When those in the group would come up with solutions to problems or good answers to what others asked Steven would post them to to the site as well. There are hundreds of webpages on the site with answers to most of the basic questions an RVer could ask.

While RVbasics is still a valuable resource, it was created before modern content management systems came about. Each page is created manually using HTML which makes adding new pages, managing and updating difficult. That is why we have turned our attention to RVTipOfTheDay.com. It is so much easier to make new posts and manage the site.

Any information that we add to the internet from now on will likely be posted here.

Thanks to all who have contributed to our large collection of RV Tips. This book could not have been possible without the help of everyone who contributed to helping others enjoy RVing as we all do. If we could award a gold trophy to the person posting the most on the RVBasics forum I have to say the award would go to Jim Foreman who is also a storytelling author and collector of lifetime experiences.

> *Over the years the RVclub just faded away and eventually the owner of the domain name sold it to Good Sam Club.

About RV Quick Tips

There are many RV Quick Tips… just one or two sentences long which don't require any elaboration... included in the book. These RV Quick Tips may or may not be relevant to the sections they are in because we simply fit them in wherever space would allow.

We know you will find them valuable.

Links to World Wide Web Resources

Where appropriate we have included Web links to products, services and additional information. There are two inherent problems with including web links in a printed book... 1) link addresses have to be manually typed into a web browser which can be a pain if they are long. 2) link address sometimes become obsolete but cannot be changed until the next book update.

We try to mitigate these problems by using a webpage to keep up-to-date, clickable links at **http://RVTipOfTheDay.com/links**

Table of Contents

Table of Contents

RV Camping Tips 29

RV Travel & Destination Tips 42

RV Driving Tips 52

RV Weight Ratings and Weighing Your RV.......78

RV Lifestyle Tips 88

Fran took this photo of our current rig at a rest stop on
I-70 in Utah during a cross country trip in 2009.

Our first fifth wheel parked in front of the
Judge Roy Bean Visitor Center, Langtry Texas 2004

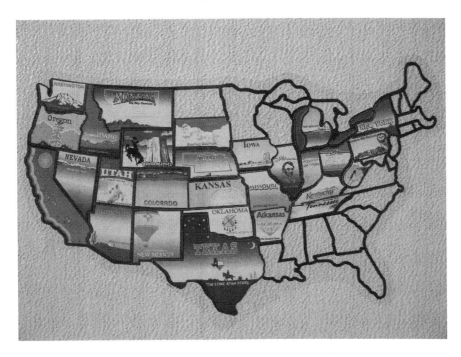

Haven't filled in all the states yet but we're working on it.

RV Care & Maintenance Tips

RV Washing Tips

- Work in the shade if possible or wash early in the morning before the temperature gets too hot. A hot surface causes the wash and rinse water to evaporate too quickly increasing the likelihood of water spotting.

- Park on a slight incline to allow rinse water to run off moldings, trim, and recessed areas better.

- Wash tires & wheels first. If you clean the RV first, when you wash the wheels you'll probably spatter cleaners, dirt and brake dust on already cleaned panels around the wheel wells.

- Start by thoroughly wetting the RV with a medium spray of water to remove loose grit and surface dirt.

- Wash from the top down and rinse the RV often. Frequent rinsing is especially important.

- Use a detergent specifically formulated for automotive or RV use. Follow the directions on the bottle for the proper mix ratio. Using too much soap is wasteful and may leave a soap residue on the surface.

- Most RVers use a scrub brush with an extension handle. You will want one with soft bristles, and lots of them, so the brush will hold a lot of soapy water.

- Sheepskin wash mitts keep grit away from the surface and should last for years. 100% cotton chenille wash mitts and pads are also excellent but will need to be replaced from time to time.

- WD-40 can serve as an alternative to commercial bug & tar remover on the oily road buildup that accumulates on the lower panels of your RV. Wash the RV as usual after application.

- To clean tough spots on your windows, wipe down with rubbing alcohol, allow to dry, then clean as usual.

- Renew your windshield wiper blades by cleaning with a low-abrasion scouring powder then wiping them with rubbing alcohol. Makes the wipers last longer and stops them from streaking.

- A child's wax crayon, close to the same color, makes an effective repair to tiny scratches on your paint. Rub the crayon over the scratch, then buff smooth with a clean cloth.

Wash & Wax Without Water

As a full time RVer it's tough to keep the RV clean. With so many RV parks not allowing washing on site it can be a long time between wash jobs.

Some years ago there was a product being pitched to RVers that let you wash your rig without water. Just spray it on, wipe clean and buff to a shine.

To the RVer, the product's primary appeal is that you can wash your rig without violating no-wash rules. Although I have not seen this product mentioned in RV circles in quite a while it's still available. My only complaint is that it's expensive.

I've discovered that you can make something that works very well at a fraction of the price. All you need is a spray bottle, liquid automotive wash & wax and just enough water to get some wetting action going. I've used liquid Simonize 500 Series but only because I got a half gallon at Sam's Club at a good price. Your favorite brand of liquid should do fine.

Because wash & wax products are different you'll have to experiment to determine the best mix of product to water. The mix really isn't critical so start with a 50-50 mix and adjust from there as you use it and see how it does.

Once you have your spray bottle in hand choose a starting point and work on one section at a time. Spray the area and clean with a damp...not wet...cloth. Rinse the cloth often enough to keep it clean. Give the wax in the product a chance to dry then buff with a clean dry cloth.

I think you'll be surprised at how well it cleans and the wax job is far superior to the typical wash job. Furthermore I've never heard of an RVer being expelled from an RV park for 'waxing' their rig.

Keep Your Gelcoat Looking Like New

The outer surface of a fiberglass panel is normally a special resin called gelcoat. The cosmetic component of the laminate gelcoat provides little structural value.

When gelcoat is sprayed into a mold it takes on the shape and texture of the mold surface. The glossiness of gelcoat is due entirely to the highly polished, surface of the mold.

Exposure eventually erodes the surface of gelcoat, leaving it dull and chalky. Fortunately, the gloss can usually be restored.

On a new RV, routinely waxed gelcoat can retain its gloss for 15 years or more. The primary purpose of wax is to protect, but wax also has restorative properties.

Here's some tips for keeping your gelcoat looking like new.

- The first step in restoring the gloss to gelcoat is a thorough cleaning. A cup of detergent to a gallon of water is a good cleaning agent. If mildew is present, add a cup of household bleach to your cleaning solution. Difficult stains may require direct application of a concentrated cleaner formulated for fiberglass.

- Rinse the clean surface thoroughly and let it dry.

- For dependable results from wax or polish, the gelcoat surface must be free of oil and grease. After washing, wipe the surface with a rag soaked in MEK (preferred) or acetone, turning the rag often and replacing it when you run out of clean areas. Protect your skin with thick rubber gloves.

- When applying wax you should follow the manufacture's application instructions, but usually wax is applied with a cloth or foam pad using a circular motion. Let the wax dry to a haze, then buff away the excess with a soft cloth. The remaining wax fills microscopic pitting in the gelcoat and provides a new, smooth, glossy surface.

- An electric buffer can take much of the work out of keeping your RV shining but keep in mind they operate at relatively slow speeds, don't try to "make do" with a polishing bonnet fitted to a disk sander or chucked into a drill. You will probably ruin the gelcoat surface.

Before relying on this information you should contact the manufacturer for recommendations for your specific RV. If that's not possible consult an auto body or RV tech. Also note that a surface that looks like gelcoat may not be.

RV Rubber Roof Care & Preventing White Streaks

RVs with rubber roofs may get white streaks caused by the natural oxidation of the rubber roofing material. You can minimize white streaks by washing the roof twice a year.

Keep in mind when you are washing a rubber roof that the oxidation on the surface acts as a barrier to further oxidation of the rubber below so your goal is not to eliminate all the oxidized material but only to remove the chalk or powder buildup that will cause the white streaks down the sides of your RV.

To maximize the life of your roof use a soft brush (the same one you use to wash the rest of the RV should do) and avoid excessive scrubbing.

Beware of Black Streaks

Black streaks down the sides of your rig are caused by run-off from the dirt, bird droppings, fallen leaves and other stuff that decays and is washed off the roof of your RV during light rains and heavy dew. Regular cleaning of your roof, especially just before the rainy season starts, will go a long way toward eliminating the cause of black streaks.

You may want to clean your RV's roof more often than twice a year if you regularly park under sap dripping trees, fruit trees, trees that attract a large bird population or places where harsh environmental fallout may settle on your roof. If allowed to stay on your rig for an extended period of time these conditions may result in unremovable stains.

Washing the sides of your RV with a good wash & wax product regularly will do a lot to keep rooftop-black-streak-causing stuff from building up on the sides of the rig.

If you already have a black streak problem try WD-40 before you go out and buy some special cleaner. You'll have to wash with regular soap and water after using WD-40.

Beware of some cleaning products…they may permanently remove the gloss from fiberglass RVs. Always test a small, out-of-the-way place first. Gel Gloss will clean black streaks from most fiberglass.

Some people use common bug and tar remover. Turtle Wax makes one as do many other companies. Again try it on a small out-of-the-way place first.

RV Decal & Graphics Tips

Larry Housell of Rialta Graphics offers some tips for keeping RV graphics in good condition and for removing old graphics.

The care of decals is simple. Keep wax and cleaning agents away from the decal edges.

When washing the decal dry the edges of the decals well as the adhesive tends to fail by reacting with other chemicals.

Use a UV protecter on the face of the decal, I use a small, foam brush and spray the brush and wipe the decal trying to stay close to the edge.

There are two basic types of vinyl used to make decals:

- Calendared has a 3-5 year life span

- Cast has a 5-9 year life span

The cast vinyl will cost more of course but is nearly always worth the extra expense.

A large number of decals used on RVs are printed using a solvent based ink, and most times have a UV shield installed. These normally have a white border. Some decals are silk screened using permanent inks.

The cost of replacing decals can be high. Design time adds a lot to the cost, for example, if the decal does not use a standard font. In addition, the number of decals ordered has an impact on the cost; the more you order the cheaper each one should be.

If the time comes you have to remove a decal, do not use a heat gun. A heat gun would be too hot. Use a hair dryer on the low setting and don't get too close to the decal. The idea is to soften the adhesive, then use an old credit card to slide under the edge and work in under the decal softly.

I recommend an orange-oil based cleaner to remove the residual adhesive.

Before applying a new decal use a soft cloth and rubbing alcohol (Isopropyl) to remove any residue. Then wash and allow the area to dry. You may want to use the wet application technique depending on the complexity of the new decal design.

A sign shop that produces vinyl decals might be able to provide a small amount of vinyl sealer which when applied will help prevent the decal from peeling.

RV Awning Care & Maintenance Tips

- Your patio awning will last years if you do a little preventive maintenance and cleaning.

- When you open the awning for the first time after it has been stored for a while, inspect the awning fabric for any signs of mildew or stains. If the awning fabric is fairly clean, normal cleaning can be done with a soft brush and mild soap and water. More difficult stains, or mildew, can usually be removed with a 'soft scrub' type household cleaner.

- Clean and rinse both sides of the awning and allow it to dry completely before rolling it up.

- The fabric used on most awnings is made from vinyl but some are acrylic.

- Once the awning fabric is clean, inspect it for punctures and tears. Small pinholes can be 'plugged' with a dab of vinyl adhesive. Larger punctures and rips can be patched with a vinyl repair kit available at RV repair centers.

- If you happen to have acrylic fabric, use a dab of clear silicone sealant to plug pinholes. For punctures and rips, get a scrap of matching fabric from the manufacturer to use as a patch and use clear silicone to adhere the patch on one or both sides.

- Clean the awning hardware with the same cleaner you use to wash the RV. While the awning is out, inspect the awning hardware. The bottom awning brackets support most of the weight of the awning so it's important to check that the lag screws are tight.

- A bent roller tube will be noticeable when you roll the awning in and out. Inspect all hardware for proper operation and broken rivets.

- The spring tension on the roller tube is very strong and can result in serious injury if you attempt to remove the awning end caps. Unless you know how to do it properly, let an RV tech do the work.

- Make sure the awning rail is securely mounted to the side of the RV. Check that all screws are tight and properly caulked.

Here are some things to remember when using the awning.

- Wind speeds over 20 miles per hour can cause damage to the awning and your RV. Of course you can never know when a strong wind gust may blow through but you can minimize the chance for damage by never leaving the awning out when you're not using it.

- You can also use awning tie downs to help prevent damage caused by sudden wind gusts or storms.

- For those breezy days, awning de-flappers really work.

- If your awning is long and flaps in a breeze consider adding a center rafter. The tension it puts on the center of the roller tube keeps the awning pulled tight and minimizes flapping.

- The weight of rain water pooling on your awning can cause costly damage. Lower one end of the awning to allow for water runoff.

Have you ever grabbed your awning rod and reached up to pull the awning strap and the loop was nowhere to be seen? If you haven't yet you probably will. You could get a ladder and reach up and feel for it...it's there somewhere...or you can skip climbing the ladder and do it this way:

- Make sure the awning ratchet lever is pulled down and the travel locks are released, use the awning wand to hook onto the axle between the roller tube and the support arm. Pull down and out like you would pull the strap. You may have to alternately pull both ends of the awning until the strap reappears. When you can hook the strap, roll out the awning as usual. If you can't reach the axle you can just pull out on the awning support arms.

- A too-long awning strap is another problem. Trust me you don't want to listen to the strap loop tapping on the side of the rig all night when the weather is windy. I have a good idea how Edgar Allen Poe really felt about that raven! The strap can also, over time, wear the finish of the wall from constant rubbing.

- If you have a long awning strap, the next time you roll the awing in let the strap roll up at a slight angle. Doing so will wrap more strap with each roll of the awning. You may have to experiment with different angles to get it to roll up just right, but it works.

Tips for Taking Your RV in for Repairs

Even if you pride yourself on being able to do your own RV repairs there will be a time when you'll have to take your home on wheels to the shop for repairs. Here are some tips to help insure you have a positive experience:

- Use your warranty. If your RV is new, take full advantage of your warranty period. There will be repair issues that become apparent as you use the RV. Keep notes and allow plenty of time to get these items resolved within the warranty period.

- Know who is paying. Know what is covered, and not covered, under manufacturer warranties and any extended warranty policy. The RV service department usually will not start the work until it is clear who is paying the bill.

- The extended warranty company will likely have a labor guide or they may use a manufacturer's labor guide that indicates the total hours it should take to diagnosis and make the repair. They may also have a maximum labor rate. Be sure you and the service department are aware of this and if the service department will bill the job accordingly.

- Plan ahead. You can't plan for emergency service work, but when possible plan service appointments well ahead of time. Most RV service centers are booked ahead and during the RV season you may have to wait several weeks. Even if they can get your RV in quickly, parts may need to be ordered which can take weeks to arrive. Check with your service center.

- Prioritize your work. Make a list of the work you want done in order of priority. A prioritized list is especially important if you have a time limit for repairs or a limited budget. If the RV service center rewrites your list to their own form, be sure you compare their version with your list.

- Fix the problem not the symptom. Make sure you and the service manager understand the cause of the problem before you agree on how it will be repaired. Otherwise you may end up spending time and money treating symptoms while continuing to have problems.

- Follow up. Ask the service manager for an estimate of when the work will be completed and then keep track of what work is being done and if the work is still on track. Make sure the service manager has a contact phone number but don't rely on him to call you, a service manager often has a large number of customer demands to juggle and it's easy to overlook things. You don't want to make a pest of yourself but a good RV service manager should be willing to give you progress reports.

- Be flexible. Repairs may take longer than initially expected. Allow some flexibility in the travel plans or appointments you schedule following the repair work. The repair work may also cost more than estimated so having a special fund for RV repairs can help with unforeseen expenses.

- Use the 'downtime' well. RV service centers usually have a waiting room, and it can be enjoyable spending time there chatting with fellow RVers about the RV lifestyle and picking up tips. If you are at a service center that does much work on your brand, the tips and ideas may be especially helpful. When the service work will take most of the day you can take a long lunch and/or spend time out exploring local sights.

- Take a vacation. If you are a full timer or extended traveler you may have to vacate your home on wheels for a few days depending on the extent of the RV service work. Why not plan a cruise, take a plane trip back 'home' or just spend a few nights in a bed and breakfast inn.

- Inspect the work. Before you drive away from the service center do a thorough inspection to insure all work has been completed and been done properly.

Windshield Wiper Blade Care Tips

Visibility is fundamental to safe driving. Even though drivers depend on their wiper blades to clear away rain, sleet and snow, many wait to replace them until they need them the most. So remembering to maintain wiper blades regularly can maximize visibility, efficiency and reliability.

Avoid problems and extend the life of your wiper blades by following these simple steps:

- Clean your windshield often and at least every time you fill your gas tank.

- Gently wipe the rubber squeegee with a damp paper towel to remove any loose dirt or oil.

- Never use your windshield wipers to de-ice your windshield. Instead, either use an ice scraper or use your defroster to melt snow and ice.

- Pull your wiper blades away from the windshield during winter months to prevent ice build up on the rubber squeegee and to prevent them from sticking to the windshield.

- Wiper blades should be replaced every year or as soon as you notice a squeak, chatter, skip, smear or streak reducing driving visibility.

- An easy way to remember to proactively change your wiper blades is to replace them at same time each year. Pick a birthday or other special date that coincides with the beginning of the rainy season.

When inspecting wiper blades, look for the following:

- Broken frame – detachment of frame arms at joints or connection points

- Metal Corrosion – especially at joints and claws

- All joints hinge freely

- Visible cracks, tears, and missing pieces in the rubber squeegee's edge

- Flex rubber squeegee back and forth to see if it is still flexible. Aged squeegees will have difficulty conforming to the shape of your windshield and create streaks.

- Check the squeegee's wiping edge for rounded edges which can prevent the wiper blade from making proper contact with the windshield

- Ensure wiper blades have been securely installed on the wiper frame

- If the frame assemblies are in good condition you can save yourself a few dollars by just replacing the rubber squeegee with a refill. Remember to check your wiper blades as part of your regular preventive maintenance program.

The Importance Of Tire And Wheel Balancing

To get optimum tire performance from your RV tires, the weight of the tire and wheel assembly must be properly balanced. Out-of-balance tires tend to cup and wear excessively at the heavy spot. You should have wheel balancing performed when:

- New or used tires are mounted on wheels.

- A tire and wheel are moved to another position.

- A flat has been repaired or replaced.

Tire Rotation Patterns

Every motor home and trailer is unique, so consult your owner's manual for rotation recommendations for your vehicle. If the tires on your vehicle show uneven wear, ask your tire professional for advice.

Wheel Alignment

Proper wheel alignment is essential to maintaining even tread wear on your RV tires. Normal wear of moving parts in a suspension system can result in misalignment, which can cause scuffing and rapid, uneven wear. Motor homes should have regular alignment checks and adjustments.

Routine Tire Inspections

Thoroughly inspect your tires at least once a year. It's also a good idea to inspect them after you drive on rugged, rocky terrain or when you take your RV in for service. Check both sidewalls, the tread area, valves, caps and any valve extensions. Look for nails, cuts, bulges, aging, cracks and weathering, as well as objects lodged between the duals.

Cleaning RV Tires

Cleaning RV tires is a yearly necessity. Dirt, road tar, and debris can all build up on your RV tires and lead to deterioration of the rubber. Use a soft brush and cleaner formulated for tires to clean the road grime from your tires and wheels.

Beware of tire "dressing" products. Many of these products contain petroleum or petroleum derivatives that can definitely speed up the deterioration of your tires or cause them to crack too soon. RV tires usually don't get as much milage on them compared to passenger car tires so it's more likely you'll have to replace them due to age and cracking rather than tread wear.

RV Quick Tip

✱   A five gallon bucket makes a good storage container for your sewer hose. You can store a 10 foot hose with fittings by coiling the hose with the fittings in the center of the coil.

Shoe Polish Restores Plastic Trim

The way tips are shared across the internet, and with my poor memory, I cannot give credit to whoever thought of this tip. I wish I could say I thought of it.

Do you have an older RV or vehicle with black plastic trim that is faded and gray? Try Kiwi shoe polish. When I first heard about it I was skeptical but I have tried so many other products to 'restore' the plastic trim on my truck that didn't work I thought why not try it?

I do have to say that I had mixed results but overall I think shoe polish works quite well. Much better that the other products.

The bumper trim on my 1996 truck was in bad shape, part of the trim was gray and the part that was still black was dull.

It took three applications over three evenings to get it looking reasonably good but it needs a couple more coats of polish to even out the shine…it's an old truck.

I had much better results with the plastic trim around the taillight assembly. I think because that plastic is different… harder…it only took one application of the shoe polish to bring it back to like-new condition.

I believe the shoe polish works so well compared to other products I've used because it has pigment as well as polishing agents.

Get Rid of Ants in Your RV

Black ants. Cabillions of them. We got 'em at an RV Park in California and took them on a tour of the southwest before my son in Lancaster, CA suggested we use Terro. The product comes in an orange/blue/white package. Little clear plastic pods of poison. Set the pods around your RV where you've seen ants.

Some of the ants just eat the poison and die right there but many take the liquid back to their nests to share, quickly killing off the whole nest of their relatives.

Terro also comes as a powder in a dispenser bag for outdoor use around your rig or your yard or wherever ants may be. We got our Terro at WalMart… the liquid type in the pest control section of the grocery department and the bagged powder type in the garden department. It's not a WalMart brand product so it is probably available in other stores. It worked for us.

Here's some tips offered by members of the RVbasics Yahoo Group:

- A rag…an old sock works well…soaked with diesel, Raid or PineSol wrapped around power cable, water hose, TV cables etc will stop ants and other pests from entering your RV.

- PineSol in a spray bottle with about a 1:3 mix with water kills them dead. And it removes the scent trail they leave so others can follow them.

- Don't forget to spray or apply powder around landing gear and leveling jacks.

- Tree branches and bushes that touch your RV as well as tall grass under your rig will also provide a bridge for pests.

- Carol says: We store our pop-up at a KOA. Twice we've had the invasion! What do you recommend for while the unit is in storage in an open field?

- Steven says: Get yourself a small garden sprayer and a gallon of liquid pest control and saturate the underside of trailer. You can also get jugs of liquid with a sprayer included.

- When parking for storage, spray around tires and leveling jacks, anything that touches the ground. It helps if the grass is cut so as not to provide a path into the RV. Trim away any tree branches that may hang down and touch the roof of the RV as they can also provide a path for ants and other bugs.

How to Deal with Condensation in Your RV

As a youngster, waking up at my house and finding the windows steamed up meant mostly one thing…it was Thanksgiving or Christmas!! My folks would stuff a huge turkey late the night before a holiday and put it in the oven at a low temperature to cook slowly. By morning the warm air and moisture had filled the house. It smelled so gooood …and moisture condensed on the windows since the air outside was very cold.

Condensation in RVs could lead to more problems than just being unable to see out windshields and other windows. If it runs from the window frames, seeps into cracks and crevices it could spawn molds to which many people are allergic. Therefore it would be good to find the source and go about abating it.

Possible sources of warm moist air: furnaces or heaters, a number of people and pets breathing out, ovens, ranges and coffeepots, baths and/or showers, washing/rinsing dishes, etc. When it is very cold outside and a combination of these things is occurring inside condensation is likely to form. This is normal.

Here are a few tips for dealing with condensation:

- Dehumidifiers come in many sizes and price ranges, and take up space. GOOGLE dehumidifiers and consider the pros and cons for your situation.

- Crack open a window or vent in the bathroom during showers and in the kitchen area while cooking. If you need to drive a motorhome early in the day…don't shower in the morning.

- Allow a small opening in a window or two at night. (No, a bit of escaping moist heat will not affect global warming.)

- There are products that keep windows and bathroom mirrors from steaming up. They come as spray and wipes, or just a cloth that you wipe over the windows. Some of them are available in auto parts stores or WalMart.

- There is also a product I remember from SCUBA days. It comes in a pound or half pound container and is pink. It may be called Pink Magic…I can't remember. A gob of it spread over the inside of a SCUBA mask kept the glass clear in cold water. I think a coat of it on the inside of an RV windshield would help keep condensation under control. Yes… it had another name, but I can't make my fingers type that here.

RV Quick Tips

✱ Local cuisine is a special treat. Budget for meals out. Ask locals where the best places to eat are.

✱ I like to use a 4-way lug wrench for trailer tire changing because it offers a lot more leverage. But it almost always took me four tries to find the socket that fits the lug nuts until I spray painted the correct one. If you don't have paint you can just wrap a length of tape at the end of the shaft near the socket.

Boondocking – Dry-Camping – Overnighting Tips

The term boondocking is often loosely used by RVers to describe any 'camping' outside of RV parks and designated campgrounds. Boondocking usually implies dry-camping… camping without hook-ups. Because the term is used so loosely it sometimes causes confusion, especially among RV newbies.

What is Boondocking?

Boondock is defined as backwoods, backcountry, middle of nowhere, wasteland, bush; informally as boonies, sticks. So, in it's strictest definition "boondocking" is camping in the "boondocks." This type of camping is usually on public lands…state and national forests, Bureau of Land Management (BLM) lands, etc. and is free or very low cost. In boondocking areas there are usually no developed facilities and never any hook-ups. Rules are mostly relaxed…based on civility and consideration of others and the environment.

What is Dry-Camping?

Dry-camping means camping without hook-ups. No water, electricity, or sewer hookups but rather using your RV's ability to be self-contained. You might dry-camp in a city park, a state or federal campground, a private RV park, a relative's driveway or a parking lot.

What is Overnighting?

Overnighting refers to short 'overnight' stays at places other than campgrounds and RV parks… WalMart and Flying J parking lots being examples. When overnighting, RVers are usually dry-camping but rarely boondocking.

Of course, when used together with RV, the word 'camping' creates nearly as much confusion, and often heated debate, but we'll cover that another time.

Boondocking Gives Your RVing Budget a Break

RV travel is among the least expensive lifestyles and there are many ways to make RVing fit even the most frugal budget.

One of the best ways to save money when RVing on a budget is to boondock on Bureau of Land Management (BLM) land. There are many places to boondock even for extended stays. The ones that I'm most familiar with are the BLM lands in western Arizona around Quartzsite and Yuma, and southern California at Slab City near Niland. But there are many others around the country.

A Google.com search for 'free boondocking areas' will find more places and information. Also, easy on the budget overnights can be found in parking lots, relative's driveways and some RV parks or campgrounds that have dry camp areas. These are usually very low cost or free.

Boondocking & Dry-Camping Tips

Some of the most beautiful places RVers can visit don't have a campground. Even in places where there is a campground the sites may not have hookups. That's okay because almost all RVs are made for dry-camping.

The easiest way to practice dry camping is at a campground with hookups, only don't hook up. Instead try to dry-camp as long as you can following the tips below.

Then, if you run out of fresh water and your holding tanks fill up, you won't have to drive to a dump station. If your batteries need charging you can just plug in.

Once your batteries are charged, you've refilled the fresh water tank and emptied the black and gray tanks, unhook again and try to prolong the time. If you can dry-camp for at least a few days you're ready to try real boondocking.

Water Use Conservation Tips

- Your black and gray tanks should be empty and your fresh water tank should be full when you reach your campsite.

- Take along one or more portable containers of fresh water.

- Being careful with your water use is the only way keep from needing to dump waste water tanks too soon.

- When boondocking, the gray water tank usually fills before the black tank does. You can extend your stay a little longer by disposing of gray water (such as dish water) in the toilet.

- While waiting for the shower or sink water to get hot, save the cold water in a plastic dishpan or bucket for reuse such as rinsing dishes, washing hands, etc.

- When your holding tanks are full, you can dump them into a portable "blue" toter and take it to a nearby dump station. To make the best use of your time at the dump station, fill up your freshwater containers while you are there. Be sure the water is potable.

Electrical Conservation Tips

- Turn off lights, TVs and radios when not in use. Don't use more lights than necessary.

- Make the most use of daylight…getting up early and going to bed soon after dark minimizes the use of lights.

- Use rechargeable battery-operated reading lights for reading in bed, and for flashlights and lanterns outside. Keep a supply of extra batteries on hand.

- Monitor your house batteries with a digital voltmeter. (12.6+ volts = fully charged, 11.6 volts = discharged) Recharge your batteries at or before reaching 80 percent discharged, or 11.8 volts, to prolong their life.

- 120v AC appliances operating on an inverter pull a lot of power from your batteries so use them conservatively.

- Adding more house batteries will increase your storage capacity of electricity and extend your ability to dry-camp longer.

- Solar panels installed on top of your RV will help to charge house batteries to extend your boondocking time.

Boondocking Tips by Lee Turner

When I first decided to try the full time RVing lifestyle I wondered what alternatives there were to the pay-by-the-night RV campsites, the monthly leases in resort areas or Federal/State Parks. I did not like (and still don't like) the idea of being crowded in with a bunch of other campers. There are some beautiful "parks" out there, and I have stayed in some of them, but I prefer my own space and privacy to "movie night" and a community swimming pool. I also like to "move around" so what was I to do?

I found through research that many state and federal parks won't always have even basic hook ups and that you cannot use generators during certain hours. That makes sense but I love my A/C on hot nights...so what was I to do? Unless I booked with them way in advance I was probably going to have to go without hookups. Since I am a spur of the moment kind of guy making reservations just wouldn't do.

So I bought Marianne Edwards' boondocking guides and as the saying goes, "I took from them what I needed and I left the rest behind." Through Marianne and her husband's experiences I opened my own mind up to all the different possibilities available to me beyond WalMart parking lots (which I am grateful for... especially when they have a lovely view) and I discovered my own ways and places to boondock.

I find if one has a good looking RV or simply keeps their older rig in decent condition, and doesn't set out a grill and/or outdoor furniture (a chair or two is okay but tables and rugs and yard decorations...not!) one can even "camp" within view of the White House...because I have.

Places and spaces most of you might think would be off limits to folks like us are surprisingly OK to camp in for a night or two while we rest up and take in the local scenery.

A security guard can be a boondockers best friend. I approach them before setting up camp and find that with a smile and a sincere interest in letting them know you won't cause them any trouble, the answer is usually "no problem." An offer of some fresh coffee could get you assigned a special place to set up camp. You'll be amazed by how often you wake up to the most incredible views and to peaceful, quite mornings, you never imagined could be had in country towns and in big cities alike. Private spaces all over the country can become available to you only if you use a little courtesy and common sense.

I have custom made, full color, laminated, "beware of the dog", "driver too tired to proceed" and "in case of emergency phone [my area code/cell number]" signs printed up that I use in my windows when parked or away from my rig. Most concerned locals will phone my cell before knocking and risking disturbing that non-existing Doberman Pincher. This gives me a moment or two to throw on my jeans and get real friendly before opening the door.

I have also had security sticks (metal broom sticks) cut in different lengths to fit all my sliding windows for those nights I don't need the A/C or want instead to enjoying the refreshing breeze.

The reality is that most local authorities and neighborhood watch groups knock on our doors not to make us leave but to make sure we boondockers are "OK in there?" I am rarely asked to move my rig and this is true even when I am parked in obvious (and usually posted) 'no overnight or anytime parking' areas. Let's face it, no one wants the "tired" driver of a 40' anything out on the open road.

I have paid for water fill-ups and sewage/gray dumps exactly 4 times in 3 years and I spend about 300 days a year "on the road"… this can be done right and right cheaply too!

Right now (as I type) I am enjoying my morning cup of "java" while looking out at a beautiful view of the Rockies and a couple of the "greens" of the Denver, Colorado Golf and Country Club; this "cul de sac" I found the other day is an out of the way and probably rarely used turn around of some sort and I have enjoyed it for free while parked in one of Denver's highest rent zones. Today is day three but I think I am heading up into those mountains next? I have had my fill of civilization for a while.

So use your head my friends, be gracious and friendly, and keep your rig in good shape, clean and free of clutter and my guess is you will have the same enjoyable experiences boondocking as I have enjoyed these last few years. – Lee Turner

Overnighting at WalMart & Other Places

Ask permission. There's an old RV joke about asking permission. – An RVer asks security guard at a mall if it's okay to park overnight. The guard says no. The RVer asks how about all the other RVs parked there. The guard answers, 'they didn't ask.'

The point is, use your judgment. If you see other RVers there it's probably okay for you to park too. If you're the only one and your not sure, it's best to ask permission. You really don't want security or the police to knock on your door telling you to move in the middle of the night. Exercise your common sense.

Don't abuse the privilege, make it just an overnight stay and for only a few hours. A good guideline is that you should never stay longer than 12 hours, 10 would be better. If you park at 8:00 P.M. you should be gone by 6:00 A.M. And you should leave by 10:00 A.M. regardless of how long you've been there.

If the parking lot is small you should leave before the business opens. Also keep in mind that night time is when most parking lots are swept and other landscape maintenance is done so it's always good to ask for permission to park there.

Be discreet. Please, no awnings, lawn chairs, BBQs and such. If you want to 'camp' go where camping is permitted.

Show your appreciation. If you stay overnight at a truck stop buy your fuel there. If you stay at a restaurant have dinner or breakfast or both. You get the idea.

Casinos Let You Stay & Play

Few things spark the interest of RVers like free overnight parking. Places such as WalMart parking lots, and truck stops are some of the more well-known free overnight camping locations.

It is not a well-known option yet, but RVers are gradually gaining awareness of the free parking opportunities at casinos. Some offer free RV dump stations and even RV hookups. You'll find that most casinos will allow free overnight RV parking though they generally limit your stay. A few Casinos require that you be a customer to park.

There are casinos that do not allow overnight parking at all, while others request that you park at their adjoining RV campground at customary nightly rates. Since casinos are generally near populated areas a drawback could be traffic sounds from nearby freeways and busy highways.

If you have moral objections to gambling this may not be the RV parking opportunity for you. However, many of the RVers who overnight at casinos have no interest in gambling and never go inside, or just take advantage of the casino restaurant or buffet.

Add casino parking to your list of free RV overnighting opportunities. Stop, enjoy the food and entertainment for a couple of hours, get a good night's rest, then head on to your next destination.

RV Quick Tip

✱ A lot of places won't allow RVers to wash RVs in their parks. Too much water and mess. You can get a four tube pack of Clorox sanitary wipes and a 350 count box of Shop Towels at Sam's for about $20.00. Put on some rubber gloves, set out a garbage bag and wipe away. Wipe with a cleaner cloth and dry/buff with the shop towels.

Camping on BLM Land at Quartzsite, AZ

During the busy, October to April, season for RVers visiting Quartzsite it can be nearly impossible to find a site in an RV park so most RVers plan to dry camp in the desert on BLM land.

If you are planning to stay in Quartzsite for just a few days you will probably want to stay in one of the free camping areas.Quartzsite BLM – Free Camping

Free camping not to exceed 14 days in a 28-day period is permitted in non-fee Quartzsite BLM areas:

- Plomosa Road: Take 95 north from Quartzsite to the Plomosa Road turnoff. The free camping areas are on the north and the south sides of Plomosa Road.

- Hi Jolly/MM112: Head about 3 miles north of Quartzsite on highway 95 at mile marker 112 on the right side.

- Dome Rock Mountain: West from Quartzsite about 6 miles. Take I-10 west to the Dome Rock exit. Camping is south of the Frontage Road (Kuehn Street).

- Scaddan Wash: About 3.5 miles east of Quartzsite. Take the I-10 Frontage Road from mile marker 19 exit east. The camping area is south of the Frontage Road (Kuehn Street).

- Road Runner: This Quartzsite BLM camping area is on the west side of US 95, about 5 miles south at mile marker 99 on US Highway 95.

Quartzsite BLM – Long Term Visitor Areas

Planning to stay in Quartzsite for a while? Your best bet is to camp in the La Posa Long Term Visitor Area (LTVA). You'll find it south of I-10, and running on both sides of Route 95.

FACILITIES PROVIDED: 10 vault toilets (handicap accessible), dry dump station, dump station with water, water station (eight faucets), trash service, some paved improved roads, dance floor and ramada.

FEES / PERMITS REQUIRED: A Long Term Visitor Area Permit is required from September 15th through April 15th each season. The cost is $180.00 and is valid for up to 7 months. A Short Term Permit can be purchased for a 14-day stay. This permit is $40.00. Permits may be bought at LTVA entrances or at the BLM Yuma Field Office located at 2555 E. Gila Ridge Road in Yuma.

The La Posa LTVA is divided into 4 sections. Each has it's own entrance:

- La Posa West is just south of the RV Show Big Tent.

- Across the street from the West section is the North section of the La Posa LTVA.

- Further south along the west side of Route 95 is the entrance to the south section of La Posa LTVA.

- Across Hwy 95 from La Posa South is the Tyson Wash section.

Our home at La Posa South Quartzsite 2000

RV Camping Tips

Criteria for selecting an RV park or campground

I was asked by a new RVer what criteria was important when selecting an RV Park or Campground. Here's our list in order of importance:

- Location of the park relative to where we want to stay.

- Does the park have sites large enough for our rig? That includes length and width if slide-outs are a concern. The longer the rig the more important it is to ask before you arrive.

- Are the sites pull-thru or back-ins? If they are back-ins are they easy to back into? Wide interior roads and angled sites make backing in easier.

- Hook-ups. Full Hook-ups are defined as electric, water & sewer connections at the site.

Hook-ups in my order of importance are:

- Electric

- Water

- Sewer

- Good WiFi internet at the site.

- Other amenities like cable TV, rec-room, camp store, etc.

- Price. All the above being mostly equal then price becomes a factor when choosing between two parks.

Our order of importance may vary depending on how long we plan to stay. For example, for overnight stops pull thru sites are just a lot easier, but we may choose a back-in if we plan to stay longer and/or the site offers something special like a good view or more space. If the price is way too high we may only stay overnight and if the price is very low we may choose to extend our stay.

We use our bathroom so generally have no concern for cleanliness of the park restrooms and showers, but you may. However good ratings for cleanliness of the facilities in guidebooks and websites should indicate the overall quality of the park.

A Reader Comment:

You covered most of it well. I have encountered several campgrounds where the sites were not at all level. This can be a problem. I also don't like being next to the Interstate, especially at an On-Ramp. About every fifteen minutes or so some idiot on a loud motorcycle has to make as much noise as possible to enter the highway.

I like some shade trees, but want to have the ability for my Dish to connect. If I am going to stay for a while, which I normally do, I don't care to be parked East-West where I get a lot of hot afternoon sun coming in the front glass. I can insulate, but it is not entirely effective.

A Reader Comment:

These are the things I look for including comments from others above:

- Can I get in and out easily and is it near an interstate?

- Security (who are my neighbors and surrounding area. Are there trailers at the campsite, how well is it maintained?)

- Conditions of campsites (is it level?)

- Do they offer full hook-ups?

- Does it offer 50-amp service (although 30-amp will do)?

- Do they give discounts?

- Price

- Proximity to areas of interest.

Choosing the Best Campsite

Most times we don't get to choose our campsite. The friendly person in the RV park office usually gets to do that. Sometimes we do get to choose. Most of our Thousand Trails parks let members choose their campsites and of course when you're boondocking you have even more options.

For those times when you can pick your site here are a few thing to keep in mind.

To have shade on your 'patio' in the afternoon and evening park with the front of your RV pointing north.

- In areas that have prevailing winds you may want to park your RV so the entry door and patio are on the leeward side.

- In high winds you can minimize buffeting by parking the RV pointing into the wind.

- You may want to park away from a tree instead of under it to take advantage of the afternoon shade it casts as the sun gets lower in the sky.

- If you prefer a pull through rather than a back-in site, mention that to the manager before your site assignment is made. Most parks will try to accommodate if they can.

RV Camping Etiquette Tips

Before you settle into your RV campsite, consider these basic, common sense RV camping etiquette tips.

- Read the rules. Most RV parks & campgrounds have the same general list of rules, but some may have additional and/ or special rules.

- Don't let your dog's barking or your kid's behavior affect your neighbors.

- Respect your neighbor's space. Don't let awnings or camping gear intrude into your neighbor's space.

- Don't leave your outside lights on at night if you're not outside.

- Don't use another RVer's campsite as a shortcut to the restrooms, clubhouse, beach, etc., without permission. Consider occupied campsites as private property.

- When you arrive after hours, keep noise to a minimum. Do only what is necessary to get you through the night and finish setting up camp in the morning. This courtesy should be followed when leaving early. Prepare as much as you can the day before.

- Read the campground rules before lighting a campfire. If you do light a campfire, be considerate. Watch that the smoke from your fire doesn't adversely affect those around you.

- Leave your campsite clean. Pick up trash even if it's not yours.

The 7-C's of Camping & RVing

Whether you are visiting a state campground or commercial RV park, the camping etiquette guidelines below are meant to enhance your Camping and RVing experience.

1. Care: Care how you camp by being considerate of your fellow campers or RVers and use campground manners.

2. Caution: Be cautious in the use of camping equipment both on the road and at campsites. Improve your camping skills, knowing the right way is the safe way.

3. Courtesy: You are never so sensitive to others as when you are camping and that is why courtesy is so important. Practice politeness because it enhances the camping experience. Respect the privacy of others, control your children, leash and pick up after your dogs.

4. Cleanliness: Be clean in your camping habits and teach your children the importance of cleanliness. Pick up litter no matter who left it and be proud of the campsites you leave behind.

5. Cooperation: Observe to the letter and spirit of camping regulations and the rules established to protect your enjoyment of the outdoors. Since camping at its best is sharing, work cooperatively with others to make it better for everyone.

6. Conservation: Protect the environment in which you enjoy camping and help those whose job it is to guard and wisely manage your country's natural resources. Leave a better outdoors for those who follow us.

7. Common Sense: Apply common sense to every situation knowing that reason, understanding and humor make camping better for you and others.

RV Park Reservation & Check-In Checklists

Make sure your RV park reservations are efficiently and correctly processed and your check-ins are easy and quick.

Checklist for making RV park or campground reservations:

- Review the campground or park's website first

- Have dates of arrival and departure

- Know the width with slides out and the length of your RV including tow or towed vehicle.

- What kind of site…pull thru or back-in?

- Know your electrical needs…50 amp service or can you get by on 30 amp?

- Will you want to use WiFi or in-office internet connection?

- Have your credit card number ready

- Ask for check-in and check-out times

- Ask about special directions to the park, the best way to approach and potential highway hazards on the way in.

Checklist for RV park or campground check-in:

- Try to park to not interfere with other traffic going in or out during your check-in.

- The whole family need not go in to register. One person can handle it.

- Take your credit card, checkbook or cash and any discount cards in with you.

- If you are early, before check-out time, don't get upset if your site isn't available.

- Want to stay longer? Check with the office as soon as possible so they can try to accommodate you. Be aware that they may not be able to do so without moving you to another site if one is available.

- Ask about special rules for children, pets, use of facilities, etc.

- Find out directions to the hospital if you have medical issues.

- If you were given written information, read it. It should answer questions for you about the park and surrounding area.

Double Check Your RV Before You Leave the Campsite

Have you ever left a campsite with your TV antenna up, hatch door open, steps out, electrical cord dragging or any one of a number of goof ups?

Just before hitting the road, take one last walk around and through your RV to make sure you have put everything away properly. Switch…husband should check inside and wife should check outside. It's a matter of two sets of eyes are better than one.

When checking outside, walk out away from the RV. Doing so gives you a different perspective that may let you see something about the rig you wouldn't see otherwise. You will be able to check the roof for the TV antenna as well as for things that may be underneath the RV. Walking back a ways allows you check the campsite one last time to look for items that missed being packed.

RV Quick Tip

✱ If you have more than one key for your outside compartments paint the keys different colors and put a dab of paint on each lock that matches the key.

Emergency Campground Information

Emergencies occur without warning, even when RVing. Are you prepared?

When you pull into a campground or RV park you, no doubt, know what state and urban area you are in/near. Would you be prepared for an emergency while there? Do you have all the information you would need to summon help?

Even though you, or those with you, may not need emergency help you might need emergency information of some sort to assist a fellow RVer. When checking in ask if there is anything special you should know about what to do in case of an emergency.

You may receive some emergency information on a handout from park management when you register, but if that is not the case here are some things you should know or could ask about:

- The name and address of the campground or RV park and a nearby cross street

- Should you call 911 or contact the police or sheriff department

- What county you are in... weather reports are by county

- A park emergency number…to contact staff to meet emergency responders at the gate and direct them to the right place

- Ranger Station phone number if you are in a public campground

- Your space number and RV type

When you have lived in one place most of your life you just know all these things, but pulling into a strange location it's good to always 'Be Prepared.' Hey…it works for the Boy Scouts.

Security in RV Parks & Campgrounds

Generally speaking, we feel pretty safe in RV parks and campgrounds. In one snowbird RV park we didn't even lock our door. But there is crime in RV parks and campgrounds and it's foolish to ignore the possibility that you could be a victim.

Here's some tips to consider:

- The RV park or campground itself is the biggest factor in determining your level of security. RV parks in urban settings are probably more prone to crime than the quiet campground tucked away in the country. Don't let that make you complacent though.

- Question management about security…do they have nightly patrols? Is the park well lit? How hard is it for non-guests to come and go? Is there more than one entrance/exit?

- Get in the habit of locking your rig every time you leave your site. We had gotten so complacent about leaving the door unlocked at our favorite RV park that when we moved on we often forget to lock it. Now we just lock it every time no matter how safe we feel just to stay in the habit.

- Lock exterior storage compartments and windows.

- Lock your towed or tow vehicle.

- Close blinds and shades to make "casing the joint" harder.

- Put away any outdoor gear…cooking items, chairs, etc. … Anything you don't want to lose. This is especially important at night.

- Be aware of your surroundings.

- Consider a small fire-resistant safe for your important papers and valuables. RVs burn hot but also fast so any safe that's rated for 30 minutes or more should be fine. Of course it will have to be securely fastened to the RV or it won't be much of a theft deterrent.

National Parks – Federal Recreational Lands Passes Explained

An Interagency Pass Program was created by the Federal Lands Recreation Enhancement Act and authorized by Congress in December 2004.

Participating agencies include the National Park Service, U.S. Department of Agriculture – Forest Service, Fish and Wildlife Service, Bureau of Land Management and Bureau of Reclamation. The pass series, collectively known as the America the Beautiful – National Parks and Federal Recreational Lands Pass, is outlined below with a brief explanation of each.

America the Beautiful Annual Pass – Cost $80.

This pass is available to the general public and provides access to, and use of, Federal recreation sites that charge an Entrance or Standard Amenity Fee for a year, beginning from the date of sale. The pass admits the pass holder/s and passengers in a non-commercial vehicle at per vehicle fee areas and pass holder + 3 adults, not to exceed 4 adults, at per person fee areas. (children under 16 are admitted free) The pass can be obtained in person at the park, by calling 1-888-ASK USGS, Ext. 1 or via the Internet at http://store.usgs.gov/pass.

America the Beautiful Senior Pass – Cost $10.

This is a lifetime pass for U.S. citizens or permanent residents age 62 or over. The pass provides access to, and use of, Federal recreation sites that charge an Entrance or Standard Amenity. The pass admits the pass holder and passengers in a non-commercial vehicle at per vehicle fee areas and pass holder + 3 adults, not to exceed 4 adults, at per person fee areas (children under 16 are admitted free). The pass can only be obtained in person at the park.

The Senior Pass provides a 50 percent discount on some Expanded Amenity Fees charged for facilities and services such as camping, swimming, boat launch, and specialized interpretive services. In some cases where Expanded Amenity Fees are charged, only the pass holder will be given the 50 percent price reduction. The pass is non-transferable and generally does NOT cover or reduce special recreation permit fees or fees charged by concessionaires.

America the Beautiful Access Pass – Free.

This is a lifetime pass for U.S. citizens or permanent residents with permanent disabilities. Documentation is required to obtain the pass. Acceptable documentation includes: statement by a licensed physician; document issued by a Federal agency such as the Veteran's Administration, Social Security Disability Income or Supplemental Security Income; or document issued by a State agency such as a vocational rehabilitation agency. The pass provides access to, and use of, Federal recreation sites that charge an Entrance or Standard Amenity. The pass admits the pass holder and passengers in a non-commercial vehicle at per vehicle fee areas and pass holder + 3 adults, not to exceed 4 adults, at per person fee areas (children under 16 are admitted free). The pass can only be obtained in person at the park.

The Access Pass provides a 50 percent discount on some Expanded Amenity Fees charged for facilities and services such as camping, swimming, boat launching, and specialized interpretive services. In some cases where Expanded Amenity Fees are charged, only the pass holder will be given the 50 percent price reduction. The pass is non-transferable and generally does NOT cover or reduce special recreation permit fees or fees charged by concessionaires.

America the Beautiful Volunteer Pass – Free.

This pass is for volunteers acquiring 500 service hours on a cumulative basis. It provides access to, and use of, Federal recreation sites that charge an Entrance or Standard Amenity Fee for a year, beginning from the date of award. The pass admits the pass holder and passengers in a non-commercial vehicle at per vehicle fee areas and pass holder + 3 adults, not to exceed 4 adults, at per person fee areas (children under 16 are admitted free). Click here to learn about volunteer opportunities in the National Park Service.

Status of former pass program passes:

Golden Eagle Passport and National Parks Pass and Golden Eagle Hologram These passes have been discontinued and replaced by the America the Beautiful Annual Pass.

Golden Age Passport This pass has been discontinued and replaced by the America the Beautiful Senior Pass

Golden Access Passport This pass has been discontinued and replaced by the America the Beautiful Access Pass

All National Parks Passes, Golden Eagle, Golden Eagle Hologram, Golden Access and Golden Age Passports will continue to be honored according to the provisions of the pass.

Only paper Golden Age and Access Passports may be exchanged free of charge for new plastic passes.

RV Quick Tips

✱   While on the road, whenever you stop for any kind of break, take time to check your rig. Do a visual inspection and be sure you check the hitch, electrical umbilical, awning and especially the tires and wheels.

✱   One of the more unsightly things on an RV can be rusty streaks from the cheap screws some manufacturers use. You can get an assortment of stainless stainless steel screws at most hardware outlets. Use these to replace the exterior screws on your RV to get rid of these unsightly rust streaks.

50 amp RV Campsites Not Really Exclusive

Some RVers think that if their RV is wired for 30 amp service they cannot use campground sites wired for 50 amp service. One member of our discussion group wrote this:

Most of the places we go we just plug into the 30 amp spots. My question is, would it hurt anything if we plug into the 50 amp spots? At one of the campgrounds we want to go to the best spots are 50 amp.

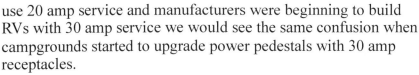

I suspect if we could remember back when most RVs were wired to use 20 amp service and manufacturers were beginning to build RVs with 30 amp service we would see the same confusion when campgrounds started to upgrade power pedestals with 30 amp receptacles.

When RV Parks and Campgrounds label a site as 50 amps it simply means the site has 50 amp service available. That is important to know for RVers who have rigs wired for 50 amps but it doesn't mean that 30 amp or even 20 amp service isn't available at the site as well. Ninety-nine percent of the time the '50 amp' power pedestal will have all three outlets... 50, 30 and 20 amp ... available.

The 50 amp and 30 amp power outlets are not the same so on the rare occasion when 30 amp service is not available you will have to use a 50 amp to 30 amp adapter if you still want use the site.

Keep in mind some parks charge extra for 50 amp sites.

RV Travel & Destination Tips

Plan Your RV Travels Using Google Maps

I've found Google Maps to be very helpful in planning our travels. It could be an acceptable substitute for having a GPS device if you use all it's features.

Google Maps is a map service provided by Google.com that you view in your web browser. You can view basic or custom maps and local business information, including business locations, contact information, and driving directions. Click and drag maps to view adjacent sections immediately. View satellite images of your desired location that you can zoom and pan.

I use it for planning the day's drive, estimating driving time and scheduling fuel stops as well as local directions for getting around in unfamiliar areas.

Google Maps gives pretty good directions but, like all mapping software, is not always perfect so it allows you to modify the route just by clicking on the blue 'route' and dragging it to your preferred route. Once you have your route the way you want it you can actually see the route using 'Street View' and even print photos of important turns and/or intersections.

Planning a stay at an unfamiliar RV Park? Use Google Maps' Satellite View to zoom in for an areal view of it. It's a good way to see what surrounds the park…industry or farmland, country lane or busy freeway. Use Street View to see the entrance and maybe some of the park too.

Again, the satellite view isn't perfect…sometimes the resolution is too low to see much when you zoom in and if the images are old then new parks won't show up. But when it works it's really nice.

Also, Street View isn't available everywhere…especially in rural or remote areas but you may be surprised at just how much of the United States Google has photographed!

The biggest drawback to depending on Google Maps is the need for an internet connection with better than dial-up speed. Fortunately many RV parks are offering Wi-Fi and if that's not available you can always visit a McDonalds or a local coffee shop.

Get started using Google Maps by going to Maps.Google.com. If you need help Google has a very complete User Guide.

Tips for Visiting Mexican Border Towns

On our RVbasics email group there was a discussion about visiting Mexican border towns. What follows is a compilation of the tips offered by group members.

Tips that will be helpful if you have never been to a border town:

- Walking across the border — Walking is the recommended way to cross the border. The streets are jammed with people walking and you just go with the flow unless you are headed for somewhere specific. If walking isn't practical it may be possible to take a taxi or charter bus.

- Riding a bicycle in border towns is not recommended. You will have to keep track of it while there and you will also be hindered by car and foot traffic. There is a good chance it will be stolen.

- Driving across the border — In border towns parking spaces are almost non-existent. If one can be found it could be on the outskirts of the town with walking distance equal to or longer than walking across the border. Keeping an eye on your car would be necessary if you like your wheel covers.

- Mexican Auto Insurance — Don't drive your car or RV into Mexico without Mexican Auto Insurance. Mexican auto insurance can be purchase on the U.S. side of the border crossing. If you are planning ahead, check with your own insurance company first, they may be able to provide Mexican insurance at a better price.

- At the crossing to Los Algodones there is a large parking lot right at the border. The shopping district is just over the border. There is a charge for parking paid as you enter the lot. There is also a RV park stateside within walking distance of the crossing. Both the parking lot and RV park are on an American Indian reservation.

- People — The people are generally wonderfully friendly and helpful. They are also persistent in trying to sell you stuff. They like to bargain. We crossed into Los Algodones so frequently when having dental work done that the vendors recognized us as we passed by and were very cordial.

- Restaurants — We stopped one day (to try out our new dental work) at a restaurant. The food was good but probably prepared more American/Mexican than 'pure' Mexican, for the tourist trade.

- Firearms and ammunition are illegal in Mexico Even one bullet in your pocket means trouble.

- English is widely spoken in border towns and U.S. currency is accepted for shopping, traveling or dining. Some dental/medical/optical accept checks on American banks.

- Returning to the United States — During tourist season one year we waited in line almost two hours to pass through the border station at Los Algonones. Usually it is not that long a wait… 20 to 30 minutes. You will need to show your U.S. passport book or passport card to re-enter. It's best not to joke around with the border agents.

- You can bring back to the States $400 worth of goods per person, plus one liter of liquor per month (this includes beer, which only amounts to about 3 cans). Hand-crafted, artistic works, are allowed in duty-free as long as you are not shipping commercial quantities. Uncooked meats and many fruits are not permitted into the U.S.

Five Tips for Safe Travel in Mexico

1. Re-insure Your Rig. The bottom line? If you plan on crossing the border in your own RV, you need to get Mexico RV insurance. In case of an accident, you probably won't be covered by your regular U.S. policy. Check with your insurance company to see if it offers a pre-approved policy in Mexico or special add-ons that will cover you within a certain mileage from the border.

2. Know the Law. In Mexico, a vehicle accident is seen as a criminal offense, and until it is determined who is at fault and whether a penalty can be paid, you could be detained in jail. Check with your insurance company to make sure they

will cover bail costs so that you aren't detained longer than absolutely necessary.

3. Stay With Your RV. Mexican law states that a vehicle must either be driven by the owner, or the owner must be in the vehicle. If the owner is not present, the vehicle will be seized by customs and not returned under any circumstances. If your name is on the title, stay with the RV at all times.

4. Plan Ahead. Know how long you will be in the country in advance. Give yourself some extra leeway in the event an accident occurs and an extended stay is unavoidable. In addition, register with the embassy, so they are aware of your presence and your whereabouts.

5. Study Up. Read your new RV insurance policy in detail and note the responsibilities you have in case of an accident or loss. Keep a copy of the policy in the vehicle at all times, and always carry your driver's license, as well – it's valid in Mexico.

The above tips provided by GMAC Insurance. GMAC works with approved Mexican insurance companies ABA Seguros and IIG to ensure that RV customers can purchase mandatory liability coverage and coverage for theft and damage to their vehicle in Mexico.

RV Quick Tip

✴   One thing I hate in a home or RV is mildew. Once it gets started, it is hard to get rid of. I keep a squeegee and a hand towel near the shower and make sure I use both before I leave. In this way there is less moisture to spur mildew on.

Travel Tips for Americans RVing in Canada

Planning an RV trip to Canada? RVing your way across Canada will be a journey of new discoveries but it is another country with different laws than we're used to here in the US.

Things not to transport in to Canada:

- Firewood – there is a ban on transporting firewood across the border. Canadian customs will not let US firewood in and the US will not let Canadian firewood in – has to do with some sort of parasite. One log can get you searched.

- Meat – you can take US beef into Canada, but unless it is clearly marked as having been purchased in the states, US Customs will confiscate beef products – to include hunter sausage, etc.

- Weapons – Canadian customs have no tolerance for anything resembling a weapon, so no guns, no brass, no ammo, nothing that even hints of a weapon, You can even got hassled over a tire billy.

- Tobacco Products – Ontario has high taxes on cigarettes so don't have a couple of cartons of Luckys laying about. You can take in enough for personal use.

The following tips are offered by Peggi McDonald, author of the book *RV Travel To Canada.*

USA and Canada are each unique but so similar. When I first began putting seminars together I was shocked to discover I had seven pages of a double space listing of differences from one side of the border to the other. Canada and United States of America co-exist on each side of the world's longest undefended border but yet we ARE two very different countries. Canadians even spell differently than Americans and sometimes we talk differently.

Canada has much less population.

However, our two countries have a mega amount in common as well. Although new Passport rules are in place as of June 09 – the good news is not much is different for RVers at the border since Homeland Security has settled into a new normalcy.

Follow these simple suggestions and your USA-Canadian Border crossing should be uneventful.

- Carry a Passport rather than the new coded style card because for Emergency Air Travel, you will need either a Nexus Card or a Passport.

- Go through the car lanes, NOT the Truck lanes.

- Some crossings have separate Bus/RV Lanes. (Note if you have wide mirrors and there are no wide lanes, talk to agents)

- Take off your sunglasses so they can see your eyes.

- Answer ONLY the questions asked – Volunteer nothing more.

- Don't be glib or smart with officials – they are only doing their job.

- Follow a 'Golden Rule Respect' with agents at the border.

- Don't try to conceal things. Officials are aware of every hiding place. Searches happen only occasionally, but they can occur while entering either country. In our 24 years of full-timing and during numerous jaunts across the border in both directions, we have only been searched once and it wasn't extensive. On one other occasion we did encounter a most difficult agent. For the most part, all of our crossings have been hassle free. These days we seem to be asked more questions than in previous crossings.

Getting a U.S. Passport Card

In preparation for a to trip to Arizona and a visit to Los Algodones, Mexico, we applied for U.S. Passport cards.

The acquisition of a passport card is not as difficult as one might imagine. Since July of 2008 these handy, credit card sized 'licenses' to get back into our native country have been available to new would-be U.S. border crossers as well as to previous passport book holders, for their renewals.

Here's a quick, step by step look at the process:

First Google passport, then choose the first website for information and application forms.

- Fill out and print, or print and fill out, the application form. Either way works.

- Acquire an original birth certificate if you haven't got one. Your birth county and/or state can provide one of these for a fee plus postage and handling if it is not local. You will get it back with your passport card.

- Get two identical photos. They are picky about this…head/face size needs to be specific and eyes need to be visible. If you choose not to have it professionally done be sure to review all the specifications for quality photos on the website.

- Take the form, birth certificate, photographs, your driver's license…oh, and your checkbook … to your county clerk's office or a post office to be processed.

- Be patient. Ours took just under three weeks. Total cost in January 2009 was $164.64 for both of our cards. It could vary some in your neck of the woods. Broken down it would be: 4 Photos... two each, $25.64, Local Birth Certificate $14.00, Distant Birth Certificate $35.00, 2 U.S.A. Submitting applications at county clerks office $50.00, fee for Passport

Cards $40.00 …Border crossing convenience …
PRICELESS.

Passport Cards are good for crossing land borders or arriving through ports of entry by ship. They cannot be used for arrivals by air.

To meet DHS's operational needs at land borders, the passport card contains a vicinity-read radio frequency identification (RFID) chip. The information on the chip points to a stored record in secure government databases. There is no personal information written to the RFID chip itself.

Places of Interest to RVers

If, in your travels, you enjoy interesting locations, unique art, or roadside attractions, these three websites will help you locate some wonderful things:

- DetourArt.com – Dedicated to the sheer joy of outsider, folk, visionary, self-taught, vernacular art and environment discoveries found all along the back roads (and side streets) around the world.

- RoadsideAmerica.com – Online guide to offbeat tourist attractions.

If you're a fan of the TV Food Network show "Diners, Drive-ins & Dives," and would like to visit some of the restaurants featured on the show, we have found these two related websites:

- www.communitywalk.com/map/326003

- www.dinersdrive-insanddives.blogspot.com

National parks are always a good choice for an RV vacation and the National Park Service website, nps.gov, is a great resource for planning your visit.

For family friendly campgrounds that offer more activities for kids, check out the Kampgrounds of America and Jellystone Parks web sites. While features at individual locations will vary, it's not hard to find a campsite that has a place for kids to swim or do crafts, or for the whole family to watch a movie under the stars .

Destination campgrounds usually have a swimming pool and planned activities to keep the whole family busy. Many also have Wi-Fi access, if you need to stay connected.

At popular family destinations, it's best to make your campsite reservation early. In some cases, as much as two to three months in advance. On holiday weekends in particular, campgrounds fill up quickly.

If you're looking for trips that will require only one tank of gas, check out the Woodall's One Tank Trip 2009 feature. This informative source describes short-distance trips in the U.S. and Canada.

Another RV camping website is Go Camping America, http:// GoCampingAmerica.com maintained by the National Association of RV Parks & Campgrounds.

RV Quick Tips

✱ For many RVers, RV travel is as much about the journey as it is about the destination. Plan to travel about six hours, or less, per day so you can enjoy the countryside and visit attractions along the way.

✱ When entering a new state, stop and take advantage of the visitor center to pick up maps and brochures. Often time you'll find discount coupons for area attractions and campgrounds.

RV Driving Tips

How US Highways are Numbered

U.S. Highways are an integrated system of roads and highways in the United States numbered within a nationwide grid.

As these highways were coordinated among the states, they are infrequently referred to as Federal Highways, but they have always been maintained by state or local governments since their initial designation in 1926.

In 1956, uniform construction standards were adopted, governing such things as access, speeds, number of lanes, width of lanes and width of shoulders.

Standards were also established for numbering the routes:

- Routes with odd numbers run north-south.

- Routes with even numbers run east-west.

- For north-south routes, the lowest numbers are in the west.

- For east-west routes, the lowest numbers are in the south.

So, I-5 runs north-south along the west coast, while I-10 runs east-west in the south.

When an interstate hits a major urban area, beltways around the city carry a three-digit number. These routes are designated with the number of the main route and an even-numbered prefix. To prevent duplication within a state, prefixes go up. For example, if I-80 runs through three cities in a state, routes around those cities would be I-280, I-480 and I-680. This system is not carried across state lines, so several cities in different states can have a beltway called I-280.

When I-95 hits metropolitan Washington, D.C., coming from the south, it becomes the famous Beltway that circles the city, signed I-495. North of the metro area, when the two circumferential highways rejoin, it becomes I-95 again.

Divided routes have been around since 1926, and designate roughly-equivalent splits of routes. For instance, U.S. Route 11 splits into U.S. Route 11E (east) and U.S. Route 11W (west) in Knoxville, Tennessee, and the routes rejoin in Bristol, Virginia. Occasionally only one of the two routes is suffixed; U.S. Route 6N in Pennsylvania does not rejoin U.S. Route 6 at its west end. AASHTO has been trying to eliminate these since 1934; its current policy is to deny approval of new ones and to eliminate existing ones.

RV Quick Tips

✽ Try to check in at your destination or overnight stop by 4pm. This will allow you to set up your camp site while it is still daylight and enjoy your supper without feeling rushed. Use the evening to meet your neighbors, explore the area or just relax and recharge for tomorrow's drive.

✽ Call to check for RV size restrictions at campgrounds before you get there. Particularly sites at state and national parks and also older private campgrounds.

✽ To conserve gray-water holding tank capacity, turn water off when shampooing and soaping up in the shower. This often referred to as a Navy shower.

Maximum Height Restrictions on Roads & Highways

When you're driving
down the road in your big
RV do you get a little
apprehensive when you see
a seemingly low overpass
or tunnel ahead? Here are
some tips to help minimize
the fear.

- Measure the height of
  your RV from the
  ground to the highest
  point on your roof...
  usually the air
  conditioner… and
  post the height on
  your dashboard so
  you can refer to it
  when on the road.

- There are minimum height standards for all state and federal
  highways. You can be sure they're higher than your RV.

- Bridges, overpasses and tunnels that do not conform to
  modern standards will almost always be signed with the
  maximum height and other restrictions (but beware, vandals
  and mother nature can remove signs). Usually there will be
  signs well in advance of the obstruction to provide a chance
  to take another route.

- Purchase a Rand McNally Motor Carriers Road Atlas Deluxe
  Edition from Amazon.com … also available at truck stops. It
  will list any low clearances and shows you which roads truck
  can go on. If a truck can make clearance, then your RV can
  go there also.

Rand McNally Motor Carriers' Road Atlas

David Carter offers this RV Tip:

We have found the Rand McNally "Motor Carriers' Road Atlas" a must have! We buy an updated version every year or two and it has NEVER let us down. It's full of neat "stuff" professional drivers need to know.

All of your questions and concerns are quickly allayed because it highlights low clearances, access and/or restricted routes due to weight, size, length, etc. While the current GPS models on the market today update themselves regularly with this essential info and other data, we find the truckers atlas handier to use than the small screen, micro keyboard GPS.

GPS devices have their place and are valuable tools, but when it comes to what route to consider, a good old quality map is the way we RVers have been traveling long before GPS hit our dashboards. — Happy Trails

General RV Driving Tips

An RV is substantially wider, longer and heavier than an automobile. These differences call for special driving procedures.

- When driving in mountains, shift to a lower gear on inclines when the automatic transmission is repeatedly up-shifting and down-shifting. The proper way to descend a grade is to shift the transmission into low gear and avoid overuse of the brakes. If at any time it appears the brakes are fading, stop and let the brakes cool before going on.

- When driving on gravel roads stay well back from vehicles ahead. Watch for oncoming traffic and slow down and pull as far to the right as possible to avoid dents or windshield damage.

- Check your mirrors every 30 seconds. Be aware of the traffic behind you and whether they are keeping up with you, passing or falling back.

- When several vehicles collect behind your RV, pull off the road at a safe place to let the cars go by. Not only is this common courtesy it is also the law in many states.

- When the temperature drops, driving conditions change. Wet roads become icy and dangerous black ice is difficult to see.

- Wearing a safety belt is the single most effective thing you can do to prevent serious injury and death in a traffic accident. Besides, it's the LAW.

- Keep a distance of at least 30 feet per 10 mph of speed between you and the vehicle in front of you. 30 feet x 50 MPH = 150 feet.

- When merging into traffic or changing lanes, match the speed of traffic as closely as possible. This makes it possible to enter the traffic lane into a smaller opening and is far safer than expecting the traffic to slow down or speed up for you. Conversely, watch the road far enough ahead so that you can avoid slow merging traffic.

- Save your brakes by watching far ahead for stop lights or traffic congestion then begin slowing down by simply letting of in the gas peddle and coasting.

- Limit your driving time to 5 or 6 hours a day (300 to 350 miles). Some RVers even drive less. Not only will you be more alert, but you will arrive at the campground with plenty of daylight to get set up and settled in before it gets dark. This gives you a chance to unwind, enjoy some of the campground amenities and get rested for another day of travel.

- When passing another vehicle in your RV allow plenty of room and use your turn signals to change lanes. Accelerate until you are past the other vehicle and you can see both of their headlights in your mirror. Signal your intention to return to the other lane and pull back in. Maintain your speed until you are well ahead of the vehicle you just passed.

Signal Your Intentions

Always use your RV's turn signals when you move into, through or out of traffic. In an emergency, and once you are on the side of the road, use emergency flashers, flares, or some other emergency signaling device to warn oncoming traffic.

Emergency signaling devices are even more important if you are unable to pull completely off the road away from the flow of traffic.

If a narrow shoulder does not permit your RV to be parked far enough away from traffic flow or you are on the top of a hill or around a curve in the road and oncoming drivers cannot see you, proper use of emergency signaling devices and a person flagging traffic away from the scene are important safety precautions.

RV Turning & Cornering Tips

Longer wheel bases on motorhomes and trucks towing RV trailers make it necessary to change your turning patterns. You must turn wider at intersections or the rear wheel may roll over the curb. Go further into the intersection before starting the turn and adjust your lane position to increase the turning radius.

Curves in the highway can also be tricky. Stay more to the center of the lane for right turns so the rear wheels will not move off the pavement. For a left turn or curve, stay more to the right of the lane to prevent the back of the trailer from tracking into the oncoming lane of traffic.

Recreational vehicles have a high center of gravity, so turning corners and taking curves must be done at slower speeds to prevent swaying. Slowdown before you enter the curve. Be sure you use your rearview mirrors to watch tracking and tail swing.

RV Quick Tips

* RVers like to color coordinate things and some have painted their propane tanks colors matching their RV. Dark colors more readily absorb the sun's rays and can cause the tank to overheat which may allow propane to vent through the pressure relief valve.

* The maximum pressure stamped on the sidewall of the tire is the maximum COLD pressure. Tire manufacturers factor in the greater pressures caused when the tire gets hot during use. Be sure to factor the tire's temperature when checking or adjusting tire pressure.

* When we travel, we tend not to think too much about nutrition and good diet. The last thing you want to do is spend more money upon your return on a personal trainer or weight management program to battle the holiday bulge and extra vacation pounds you have gained.

* Nothing will prevent a determined thief from breaking in, but attaching a sturdy gate hasp to the plywood bed platform and using a good padlock will make the under-bed storeage area a more secure place for valuables and important documents.

* When entering a new state, stop and take advantage of the visitor center to pick up maps and brochures. Often time you'll find discount coupons for area attractions and campgrounds.

* Consider inexpensive but thoughtful regional gifts for family and friends back home.

RV Tail-swing and Spatial Awareness

For several years our home base, whenever we we're in Yuba City, California, was the same RV park. We usually had the same site each time we returned. The site we had was in the same section where overnighters were assigned spaces.

While our site was large and even had a nice patch of grass, the overnight pull-throughs are gravel and concrete and very narrow. They are not angled which meant RVera had to make 90 degree turns into a site. On top of that, the road to the sites is narrow and has a chain link fence on the right side.

Innumerable times I looked out my window to see an RVer hug the fence while lining up to maneuver into one of those pull-thru sites, and then hear the crunch as the rear corner of the RV contacted the fence as it started the turn.

As you may figure, it happens mostly to RVers pulling longer fifth wheels and travel trailers, but long motorhomes aren't immune.

Depending on how close to the fence the RVer was driving and how tight the turn he made into the site, damage could be as light as a few embarrassing scratches to a heartbreaking separation of the fiberglass end cap from the sidewall.

The moral of this story, of course, is to always be aware of your RV's tail swing.

For motorhome drivers avoiding tail-swing problems is a matter of checking the mirrors.

RVers pulling fifth wheels and travel trailers can't rely on mirrors since tail-swing always occurs on the blind side of the rig. For them a good sense of spatial awareness is essential.

Spatial awareness is a well thought-out awareness of things in the space around your RV and of the RV's position in that space.

Anyone who drives a car has developed spatial awareness. We've learned how much space our car takes to make a U-turn and how much we can cut the steering wheel when pulling into or backing out of a parking spot.

Spatial awareness while driving your RV is developed the same way…practice. But how many of us actually practice driving our RV…as we did learning to drive a car?

The best place to practice driving your RV and develop spatial awareness is in an empty parking lot.

To better understand how tail-swing affects your rig have another driver line the RV along a straight line…a painted lane divider or gutter for example. Then as you watch from the rear, the driver should drive forward making as tight a turn as possible.

Using the line as a reference, watch how far the rear of the RV swings away from the line. Repeat the test two or three times making both left and right turns so you get a good feeling for how much the RV swings. Then change drivers to develop spatial awareness with relationship to where you are as the driver to the same line.

Of course even the most finely tuned spatial awareness is no substitute for a good spotter, so use one anytime it's practical to do so.

Basic Motorhome Driving Tips

Motorhomes are not difficult to drive but there are a few things to keep in mind that will make your travels safer and more enjoyable.

- Before driving, adjust drivers seat and steering wheel for comfort. Adjust all rear view mirrors for optimal views.

- The drivers seat is farther to the left of the center in a motorhome than in a car. This causes most drivers to drive too far to the right side of the road. Be aware of this and make the necessary adjustments.

- Know the minimum height clearance of your motor home. Be on alert for low, overhanging tree branches, carport roofs and canopies at filling stations, motels, etc.

- It takes longer for large motor homes to accelerate, slow down and stop. Keep far back from vehicles to allow more time to brake, change lanes and enter busy highways.

- The length of the motor home means its turning radius is much greater than a car. Make wide turns.

- When driving from a level surface up an incline, or vice versa, the rear of a motorhome may drag. While motorhomes are built to handle typical situations with built-in drag skids, driving slowly will minimize the possibility of damage. Very steep inclines should be avoided.

- Motor homes can be buffeted by strong crosswinds as well as air currents created by passing trucks. Slow down in high crosswinds. Anticipate and compensate for the effects of passing trucks with a firm grip on the steering wheel and awareness that the passing truck may create winds that push on your rig.

- When backing a motor home have someone watch out the back window or give directions from outside, while you view things through the side mirrors. Before backing into close quarters, the driver and spotter should get out and inspect the area behind the vehicle. By evaluating the situation before backing up, drivers can avoid accidents.

RV Quick Tip

✱ Check your mirrors every 30 seconds. Be aware of the traffic behind you and whether they are keeping up with you, passing or falling back.

More Tips for Motorhome Drivers

Fellow RVer Don Sinclair offers these Motorhome tips.

Measure the total length of your rig plus the toad from bumper to bumper. Some parking places have length restrictions and if you don't know your length, you have a problem. I keep a small card tucked into the edge of the dashboard with not only the length of my rig, but the height as well. You must know your height for things like tunnels or gates or fuel station stops.

If you have a rear view camera, turn it on, If you don't have one, get one. There are many inexpensive cameras that work wirelessly now. Then adjust the camera so you can see your toad in the viewing field. I leave my camera on all the time I am towing, for a couple of reasons.

First you can routinely check the toad to be sure it is still with you and does not have a flat tire. Flats that go unnoticed can cause a fire. Second it is very handy when you have to pass a slow moving vehicle. By glancing in the camera, you can easily see when the toad has passed the front of the slow moving vehicle and safely pull back into your lane.

Increase your stopping distance by allowing more room between you and the vehicle in front of you. Towing a toad back there weighing 3,000 lbs. or so, you need extra stopping distance.

Another very important thing: You cannot back up with a toad. If you try, you can do severe damage to your hitch. You must drive in such a manner that you never put yourself in the position of having to reverse when the toad is back there. If you make a mistake, you will have to unhook the toad, reposition the rig, drive the toad into position and hook it up again.

Enjoy your toad and enjoy the drive, but be aware that the toad is back there at all times. Visit Don's web site http://mybirdie.ca

Backing Your RV – Good Communication is the Key

We use our FRS radios when we're backing the rig and I highly recommend them. Using the radios eliminates yelling and allows much more information to be exchanged between driver and spotter. As the driver I don't normally have to say much so I turn the volume up and set the radio on the seat beside me.

If you don't want to use radios then you and your spouse should have specific signals. To avoid confusion your signals should be distinct and deliberate. Use your whole arm instead of just waving your hand. The basic signals you will need are stop, left, right, straight back and distance.

You should agree what left, right and straight mean too. Does the direction refer to which way the RV needs to go or which way the steering wheel needs to turn?

RV Quick Tips

* If you've been parked for a while it's easy to neglect the outside of the RV. Especially the 'back side'. But the back side is where your hookups are. Take some time each day to walk around the RV and check. Look for leaking water and sewer hoses and anything unusual. Check the condition of your slideout awnings. While you're at it, look under the RV for leaks, anything hanging loose, etc.

* Before leaving a campground or RV park, look around your site and pick up any trash, even if it's not yours. Leave your space as clean or cleaner than it was when you arrived.

Driving Your RV on Mountain Roads

Will your RV make it up the grade? Almost all grades, regardless of severity, will cause you to slow down.

Any grade steeper than six percent is considered extreme and requires special attention. The steeper the grade or the longer the grade and/or the heavier the load, the more you will have to use lower gears to climb and descend mountains.

When going down steep grades, gravity will tend to speed you up. You must choose an appropriate safe speed, then use a low gear and enough braking power to hold you back without letting the brakes get too hot.

Slow the RV and shift the transmission to a low gear before starting down a grade.

Use the braking effect of the engine…by shifting to lower gears… as the principal way of controlling your speed. Save your brakes so you will be able to slow or stop as required by road and traffic conditions.

Remember: Never 'ride' the brakes by keeping your foot on the brake peddle. The use of brakes on a long and/or steep downgrade should only be a supplement to the engine braking.

Once the vehicle is in the proper low gear, the following is a proper braking technique:

- Apply the brakes just hard enough to feel a definite slowdown.

- When your speed has been reduced to approximately five mph below your "safe" speed, release the brakes. (This brake application should last for about three to four seconds.)

- When your speed has increased to your "safe" speed, repeat steps 1 and 2.

- Do not drive in the fast lanes on a multiple-lane grade. Stay in the far right lane while climbing a steep grade if your motorhome or tow vehicle cannot maintain the legal speed limit.

- It would be better to drop to a lower gear and slow down rather than attempt to pass slower vehicles and tie up the faster lanes if you don't have enough power.

Reader Comment:

While towing up a 6% grade my Chevrolet 2500 (gasoline) engine usually has to down shift into 1st gear and run around 4,000 rpms. I attempt to feather the towing by lowering my speed during these extreme conditions.

As expected, with the engine running at 3800-4000 rpm both it and the transmission starts to heat up. If I get reasonably close to the red line I pull over but leave the engine running so the engine fan continues to pull cool air through the radiator. I suspect turning off the engine is not the proper thing to do as the engine may heat even higher?

The transmission fluid is routed through a cooler which is part of the radiator, so it can contribute to engine overheating if it is being worked hard. In heavy duty towing applications there is usually also an air to oil auxiliary transmission cooler.

Usually keeping the engine running at higher than normal RPM will help to get the temperature back down to a safe range more quickly.

RV Driving Tips for Extreme Weather

RVing by definition is supposed to be recreational. Ideally we should only be driving our RVs when the weather is fair. If you RV long enough you're going to run into bad weather. You may be able to control an RV in bad weather, but the safest thing to do would be to pull over and wait it out. Here are some tips for RVing in extreme wether.

Driving Your RV in High Winds

If you are driving in areas with strong winds, take special care. Crosswinds are the greatest threat because they can push a large motor home or a vehicle/trailer combination into another lane if you are not prepared. While fifth wheel RVs are affected by high crosswind it is especially true for travel trailers.

In most cases, driving slower is the best defense against strong winds. If you are towing a trailer, you should gradually apply the trailer brakes to help control a swaying trailer. Headwinds require a heavier throttle to maintain usual speeds.

If you anticipate driving in very windy areas, call and obtain local weather and road conditions. Good sources of weather information are local airports, highway patrols, state police, or ranger stations. Often, you will see signs along the highway which show radio frequencies for weather information.

Driving your RV in Snow

Always carry drive wheel and trailer wheel chains when you travel in snow country. Learn how to put them on before you need them. Chains are needed for both the tow vehicle and for one axle of a trailer. If you have a motor home with dual-rear wheels, you will need chains for one tire on each side. If both of the trailer's axles have brakes, the chains should go on the rear axle. Chains should go on the braking axle when only one axle is equipped with brakes.

Driving your RV on Ice

If you are towing a trailer on icy roads, go slowly, especially downhill. Use the lower gears. You may be able to gain additional traction for the tow vehicle by moderately releasing the tension of the load equalizing hitch to put more weight on the drive axle of the tow vehicle. Remember to readjust the hitch after the icy road condition has passed or vehicle stability may be affected during normal driving conditions.

Tips for Towing a Toad with Your Motorhome

Fellow RVer Don Sinclair offers these tips.

One of the first things you might hear from a seasoned driver towing a toad is "relax, you won't even know it's there." As you gain experience, that may become partially true as it does indeed become second nature with experience as time goes by. Don't be fooled by that statement. You MUST know it is there to drive safely.

I began hauling my toad, a 2001 Suzuki Grand Vitara 4 x 4, using the four wheels down method. If you are going to haul a toad four wheels down, in my opinion the easiest way to haul any toad, there are some things you need to learn before you embark on that first trip.

First, and foremost, choose and install a brake system in the toad. I use and love my ReadyBrake system, which is a simple surge brake set up that can be bought and installed for about $400 to $500. Never tow a toad without additional braking capability.

Then familiarize your self with hooking up and unhooking, Don't do it once and think you know how. Tow it around a place with limited traffic to start out as practice. I like to go to an industrial park on a Sunday morning for this purpose. It's quiet and with little traffic you can pull over, or into a parking lot for example.

Learn to unhook and hook up the toad under different conditions. You will encounter all kinds of different positions in the real world, so try to create some of the frequent ones for practice. Park on a slight uphill incline and unhook and hook up. I'm not talking a hill here, just a slight incline.

Then do it the opposite way so the rig is below the toad on a slight decline. You will run into these situations in a campground or a parking lot and you need to experience for yourself the way the toad behaves under these conditions.

In one case, the incline, the weight of the toad is pulling on the hitch and you may have to ease it forward slightly to pull the pins. In the other, the weight of the toad is pushing on the hitch and may have to be reversed slightly.

Also try unhooking and hooking up when the toad is at a slight angle to the motor home. You will have to do this in some campgrounds, so you might as well see what problems this can present in the quiet of a parking lot on a Sunday morning. Once you are confident that you can handle hooking and unhooking, you are better prepared for your first trip actually towing.

Also prepare a step-by-step list of the procedure you use to both hook up and unhook and then follow it every time. That way you won't leave the pins on the hood of the toad like I once did. Include starting and deactivating the braking system in this list as well.

Visit Don Sinclair's website St. Albert http://mybirdie.ca

Travel Trailer & Fifth Wheel RV Towing Tips

- Use a hitch system designed and rated for the trailer you are towing. Know how to use it properly.

- If you are new to RV towing, take time to practice towing your travel trailer or fifth wheel before driving on main roads. Most seasoned RVers recommend finding a large vacant lot and setting up some traffic cones to practice turning and backing.

- Before you leave on a trip, remember to check routes and restrictions on bridges and tunnels.

- Drive at moderate speeds. This will place less strain on your tow vehicle and RV trailer. Trailer instability (sway) is more likely to occur as speed increases.

- Avoid sudden stops and starts that can cause skidding, sliding, or jackknifing.

- Avoid sudden steering maneuvers that might create sway or undue side force on the travel trailer. Fifth wheels are less susceptible to side force sway but you should still be aware of the possibility.

- Slow down when traveling over bumpy roads, railroad crossings, and ditches.

- Make wider turns at curves and corners. Because your trailer's wheels are closer to the inside of a turn than the wheels of your tow vehicle, they are more likely to hit or ride up over curbs.

How to Hitch Up a Travel Trailer

These steps for hitching and unhitching a travel trailer are basics instructions. As you gain experience at hitching your rig, you will develop techniques that are specific to you and your rig.

If you're new to RVing we urge you to have an RV tech make sure your hitch is properly adjusted for your rig.

If you are having a new hitch installed, the installer should set up the hitch for your rig and show you how to hitch up properly and safely.

Hitching a travel trailer to a weight distribution hitch.

- Raise the trailer tongue until there is enough room for the hitch ball to go underneath the coupler.

- Back the tow vehicle until the hitch ball is under the coupler.

- Open the coupler latch mechanism and lower the coupler onto the ball just enough so the latch mechanism will close correctly. Use a padlock or hitch pin to secure the lever.

- Raise the tongue…the tow vehicle will also raise…about 3 to 4 inches with the tongue jack to make it easier to install the weight distribution spring bars.

- Insert one end of the spring bars into the hitch head.

- Lower the snap-up bracket (sometimes called the saddle) and place the proper chain link onto the hook.

- If you have the Dual-cam hitch setup, rest the spring bars on the ends of the cam.

- Using a short piece of pipe that should have come with your snap-up brackets, raise it back up to its normal position and secure it with a safety clip.

- Repeat the above 2 steps for spring bar on the other side.

- Safety clip the snap-up brackets.

- Retract the tongue jack to allow sufficient clearance between it and the road.

- Attach the safety chains to a permanent part on the tow vehicle. Cross the chains (like an X) under the hitch to make a cradle for the coupler. This will prevent it from hitting the ground should the hitch fail. The chains should be long enough to allow the tow vehicle and trailer to turn sharply, but not so long that they can drag along the ground.

- Attach the breakaway cable to a permanent part of the tow vehicle. This should not be attached to any other part that is used to pull or support the trailer tongue, Should the receiver fail and the breakaway cable is attached to it, the trailer brakes will not activate

- Plug the trailer electrical cord into the receptacle on the tow vehicle making sure there is enough slack to allow for proper turning but so it will not drag.

- Check all lights.

- Check brake controller for proper connection…a green light or other indicator.

Unhitching a travel trailer from a weight distribution hitch.

- If you will be camping, make sure the trailer is nearly level from side to side as you can get it by placing boards or blocks under all of the tires on the low side.

- Chock the trailer tires so they won't roll.

- Disconnect the electrical cord from the tow vehicle.

- Disconnect the safety chains.

- Disconnect the breakaway cable.

- Raise the tongue high enough to take most of the weight off of the spring bars.

- Remove the safety clips from the snap-up brackets.

- Lower the bracket and release the chain. You should be careful here. If there is too much weight still on the spring bars, it could cause the lever to jerk out of your hands.

- Raise the tongue high enough to relieve most of the spring bar tension.

- Lower the tongue to put weight is on the hitch ball.

- Unlock and release the coupler latch mechanism.

- Raise the trailer tongue until the coupler is clear of the hitch ball.

- Move the tow vehicle forward away from the trailer tongue.

RV Quick Tips

✱ Carry a box of disposable gloves for use when working with sewer hoses and other dirty jobs.

✱ A water pitcher with a charcoal filter works well to take the smell and bad taste from campground water. We have used Brita and Zero brand pitchers.

How to Hitch a Fifth Wheel Trailer

I've seen people try to drive away with their 5th wheel landing gear still down. And I know people who have dropped their 5th wheel on the pickup bed because they forgot to drop the landing gear. Read It almost happened to me!
http://rvbasics.com/techtips/almost-happened-to-me.html

Following a systematic procedure each time you hitch and unhitch will minimize the chance you will have similar problems.

Fifth Wheel Hitching

- Raise or lower the 5th wheel trailer to set the 5th wheel kingpin to proper hitch height .

- Drop truck tailgate ... if you don't have a special tailgate.*

- Open locking bar on hitch.

- Back under trailer until hitch engages the fifth wheel kingpin.

- Secure hitch locking bar on the fifth wheel hitch.

- Put truck in forward gear (don't give it any fuel or acceleration)

- And 'Bump' the hitch to make sure it is locked.

- Connect umbilical cord and breakaway switch cable.

- Check fifth wheel trailer lights and brakes.

- Raise pickup truck tailgate. *

- Raise 5th wheel trailer Landing gear.

- Remove wheel chocks from trailer wheels.

Fifth Wheel Unhitching

- Pull into the site/storage, and situate the trailer where you want it.

- Chock the wheels tightly so the trailer will not move.

- Drop the fifth wheel landing gear. (important!) Do this first so you won't forget!

- Disconnect the umbilical cord and breakaway switch cable.

- Drop the truck tailgate...if you don't have a special tailgate.

- Gently put your truck into reverse... don't give it any fuel or acceleration. This effectively moves the 5th wheel kingpin off the locking bar which will allow you to easily disengage it.

- Shift in to neutral, step on brake and apply parking brake.

- Disengage the kingpin locking bar on fifth wheel hitch.

- Slowly drive away. Making sure the kingpin is clear of anything in the truck bed and the umbilical cord and breakaway cable are not snagged.

- Raise truck tailgate... if you don't have a special tailgate.

- Adjust 5th wheel height to proper front to back level.

RV Quick Tip

✱   When driving in mountains, shift to a lower gear on inclines when the automatic transmission is repeatedly up-shifting and down-shifting. The proper way to descend a grade is to shift the transmission into a lower gear to avoid overuse of the brakes. If at any time it appears the brakes are fading, stop and let the brakes cool before proceeding.

RV Trailer Brake Controllers

Modern-day RV trailers are equipped with electric brakes that require a brake controller in the tow vehicle to operate properly.

RV trailer brake controllers rely on a signal from the tow vehicle's stoplight switch to know when to apply power to the electric trailer brakes.

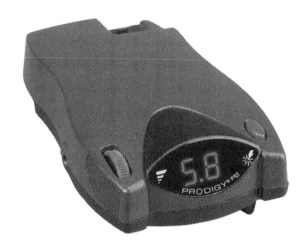

While there are many brands and models, RV trailer brake controllers are divided into two basic types — proportional and time delayed.

Proportional Trailer Brake Controllers

Proportional brake controllers, also known as pendulum brake controllers, use a pendulum as a motion-sensor to detect the tow vehicle's inertia when stopping.

When the driver applies the brakes, the pendulum swings forward and the brake controller applies power to the trailer's brakes proportional to the swing of the pendulum — if the tow vehicle is stopping quickly, the controller will apply more power to the trailer brakes. If it stops slowly the controller will apply less power.

The position of a pendulum needs to be calibrated when the brake controller is installed. When the vehicle is on a level plane the pendulum is adjusted to level independent of how the brake controller is mounted.

When properly calibrated a proportional brake controller provides very smooth braking.

Time Delayed Trailer Brake Controllers

With Time Delayed trailer brake controllers, once the brake pedal is pressed, a preset level of power…set by the user, based on trailer weight…actuates the trailer brakes.

To provide smoother braking there is a delay between the time the tow vehicle brake pedal is pushed and when power is sent to the trailer brakes. The delay can be adjusted on most time delayed controllers, but the brake controller behaves the same way each time the tow vehicle brakes are applied no matter how fast or slow the vehicle is going.

Time delayed brake controllers don't offer the smooth braking of proportional controllers and put more wear on braking systems, but they're less expensive and sometimes easier to install than proportional brake controllers.

RV Quick Tips

* Cut two pieces of foam pipe insulation… the stuff you slip it over your pipes to insulate them from the cold freezing weather… the same length as your RV's windshield wipers. Slip one of these over each of the wipers to protect them from the elements while your RV is parked. The wipers last for years this way. Just remember to remove them when you hit the road or they won't clear the windshield if it rains!

* Wearing a safety belt is the single most effective thing you can do to prevent serious injury and death in a traffic accident. Besides, it's the LAW.

RV Travel Trailer & Fifth Wheel Breakaway Switch

RV Travel trailers and fifth wheels are equipped with a breakaway switch design to apply full power to the trailer brakes should the trailer detach from the hitch and 'break away' from the tow vehicle.

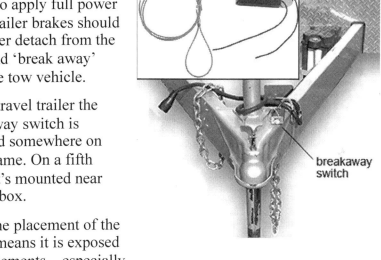

On a travel trailer the breakaway switch is mounted somewhere on the a-frame. On a fifth wheel it's mounted near the pin-box.

breakaway switch

The the placement of the switch means it is exposed to the elements...especially on a travel trailer...and should be inspected regularly to insure proper operation.

A good time to check the breakaway switch is when you are de-winterizing or otherwise getting the trailer ready for the RVing season.

Pull the pin from the housing and inspect for dirt and/or moisture. Spray a little contact cleaner into the housing to clean the contacts. Check the cable attached to the pin for weak or abraded areas and replace if necessary.

To check for proper operation of the switch jack one of the trailer wheels off the ground and spin it. While it is spinning pull the pin from the switch. If the wheel stops firmly the switch is working.

When hitching up pay attention to where and how you connect the breakaway switch cable the tow vehicle.

The cable should NOT be connected to the hitch but rather to some secure part of the tow vehicle. Make sure there is enough slack in the cable to allow for turns and make sure it cannot be snagged.

Once I spotted a fifth wheel rig parked at a gas station. It was parked in the approach to the gas pumps and the RVer was checking under the hood.

I stopped to see if I could help and the RVer said that he had just started the turn into the pumps when the brakes on the fifth wheel locked up. He wasn't sure what was wrong but had ERS on the way.

While I was talking with him I noticed the pin had been pulled out of the breakaway switch. The cable had somehow gotten snagged and when the RVer made the sharp turn to line up for the pumps the was pin pulled out.

RV Weight Ratings and Weighing Your RV

RV manufacturers provide load ratings on certification tags at various points inside or outside the RV. The certification tags are usually placed as follows (if you can't locate the sticker, check with your dealer):

- Motor homes: on door edge/pillar, or near the driver's position in the interior.

- Pickup Camper: on back exterior wall.

- Travel Trailers & Fifth Wheels: on front left-side exterior wall.

- Tow Vehicles: on driver's side door frame.

To weigh your RV, a level, commercial platform scale is needed to obtain five weights… look in the yellow pages of your local telephone directory under "Scales—Public Weighers":

- The entire vehicle with all wheels on the scale.

- Front axle with only the front wheels parked on the scale.

- Rear axle with only the rear wheels parked on the scale.

- Left side with only the left front and back wheels on the scale.

- Right side with only the right front and back wheels on the scale.

Tow Vehicle Towing Packages

When shopping for a tow vehicle keep in mind that appearances can be deceiving. For example two pickups sitting side by side on a dealer's lot may seem to be identical, except perhaps for color, but one of the trucks may have a substantially higher tow rating.

Most light truck & SUV manufacturers offer specially designed towing packages that define the equipment necessary to tow different types of trailers depending on their fully loaded weight and size. A towing package may include a heavy-duty radiator, battery, flasher system, alternator, suspension, and brakes, as well as an engine-oil cooler, transmission-oil cooler, wiring harness, specific axle ratio, and special wheels and tires.

Newer pickups may even include a trailer brake controller specially fitted into the instrument panel.

Towing packages also may include the trailer hitch receiver, which is mounted to the tow vehicle, but towing packages rarely include the draw bar, or ball mount, and hitch ball.

A manufacturer may offer different towing packages to safely tow various sizes and types of trailers. Towing packages indicate both equipment that must be installed on your tow vehicle and equipment that is optional or recommended. For example, not all trailers require the tow vehicle to be equipped with extended side-view mirrors. But if you plan to tow a trailer wider than your tow vehicle, you will need extended side-view mirrors to see rear- and side-approaching traffic.

If you already have a tow vehicle, look up its tow rating—size, maximum loaded weight, and maximum tongue weight of a trailer that the tow vehicle is capable of towing. The vehicle owner's manual contains these specifications.

Most automotive manufacturers and dealerships have towing specification guides with tow ratings and detailed information if extra equipment is needed to tow a trailer. Always insist on seeing the printed specification. Never rely on a salesman. service manager or mechanic for proper information.

While your vehicle may have certain tow ratings, remember you must have a matching hitch system that can handle the same specifications. To ensure safety, you may have to install extra towing equipment.

Travel Trailer Towing Mirrors

One thing first time RVers may have trouble getting accustomed to is using the side-mounted mirrors for rear vision. Left- and right-hand outside mirrors are required on the towing vehicle because the fifth wheel or travel trailer obstructs the driver's interior rear vision. It may appear difficult to you but with the right mirrors and a little practice you become competent using them. Side-view mirrors should be large enough and positioned for vision at least 200 feet to the rear of the vehicle.

Side mirrors should be as large as practical, with a separate convex mirror mounted below. Mount the mirrors as wide apart as possible for maximum rear vision and easy backing. Trailer towing mirrors should be adjusted so that the inside edge of the mirror is further out than the outside edge of the trailer. The travel trailer's wheels should be visible in the convex mirrors to check for correct tracking when making turns and to watch for tire problems.

Check each of your mirrors frequently for traffic conditions behind you so you can avoid last minute maneuvers and surprises. Use your mirrors to watch your trailer when making turns. Larger rigs need more space to turn without running over curbs or sideswiping stationary objects.

Travel Trailer Tire Speed Ratings

Did you know that tires have a maximum speed rating? They do. This isn't a big deal for passenger, light truck and motorhome tires because they usually have a MPH rating well above typical highway speed limits.

Nearly all Special Trailer (ST) tires used on all but the largest RV travel trailers and fifth wheels have a maximum speed rating of just 65 MPH.

Tires flex as we drive and as they flex they generate internal heat. The faster we drive the more they flex and the hotter they get. They are designed to work best within a specific range of internal heat. Too cold, they don't flex enough, too hot, they begin to fail.

When operating near or at the maximum load rating of your tires it is important to stay below the maximum speed rating since very a high internal temperature decreases the maximum carrying capacity as much as 10%. Operating at maximum speed and carrying capacity may also require a greater inflation pressure.

You can drive faster than 65 MPH but to do that you need to increase your cold inflation by about 10 psi (without exceeding the maximum PSI stamped on the tire) for every 10 MPH over 65 that you are going. You must decrease your load carrying capacity by 10% as well.

So, for example, a Carlisle ST225/75R15 Load range E (10 ply) tire, has a load carrying capacity of 2830 lbs when inflated to 80 psi when driving at 65 mph. But, when you increase your speed to 75 mph you will decrease that same tire's load carrying capacity to 2,547 lbs. That's 283 lbs less.

If you're maxing out the load rating of your trailer's tires it's imperative that you keep your speed at or below 65 MPH. Driving faster will, at the least, shorten the life of the tires and may result in tire failure while on the road.

What I'd like to have, and would be willing to pay for, is the full 2830 lbs load carrying capacity of the load range E tires and be able to drive at a more reasonable speed. Tire manufacturers should realize that RVers aren't pulling 1960's travel trailers anymore.

Don't Let That Passing Truck Sway You!

RVers who tow a travel trailer often experience a sideward push, or 'wake' of air when being passed by a truck or other large vehicle. Depending on the size of your tow vehicle and trailer, the wind conditions and the relative speed of the passing truck this sideward force can cause your trailer to sway out of control, or force your rig off the road.

You can minimize the chance for an accident by staying alert to large vehicles that may be attempting to pass you. This way you will be ready to compensate for the effects.

To reduce the sideward force and trailer sway move your rig to the right edge of your lane to make more space between your rig and the passing truck.

Proper installation and use of a sway control system will greatly reduce the effects felt from a passing truck. If your trailer hitch doesn't already have sway control consider installing one.

What size Truck?

This question and answer was originally posted at Forum.FTRV.com

Question:

I'm looking to buy a 27 ft. fifthwheel that has a GVWR of only 5171 lbs. Can I get away with a half ton truck w/gas engine? Thanks for any information you can supply.

Answer:

The answer to your question is yes, or no, and it depends.

Looking at the 2009 towing guide for Chevrolet Silverado 1500's, just for an example, depending how a truck is equipped, the max tow rating can be 4,800 lbs up to 9,000 lbs.

Much depends on what engine, transmission and differential gear ratio is built into the truck, and whether the truck is equipped with a tow package.

Never rely on or accept a salesmen's word about whether a particular truck on the lot is capable of towing your trailer. Only rely on what is printed in the manufacture's manual and other information.

Every dealer should have a brochure that provides tow ratings for all it's current truck models and what is required equipment. That's the only thing you should rely on.

If you're considering a specific truck, you need to look at the specification plate (decal) on the driver-side door pillar. It will tell you the GVRW and tow rating as well as tire pressures, paint numbers, etc., for that truck.

The dealer may be able to use the VIN to look up the specifications and an equipment package for the truck as well.

Information on tow ratings for older trucks may be available from the dealer, manufacturer or can often be found online.

RV Quick Tips

- Ensure a healthy, balanced eating style, habit and choices, with the occasional indulgence and treat as opposed to throwing all caution into the wind and making it all about the food. There are so many other activities to do, so do not let boredom drive you to the only thing most people end up doing on vacation – eating, and way too much usually.

- Never leave anything on the counters while on the road. Items secured with non-slip mats, velcro or earthquake putty may ride okay but if you have to brake suddenly or have an collision, they may come flying forward and you don't want to get knocked out by a flying toaster! Trailer owners may not have to worry about injury but do have damage concerns, If you don't want it broken, put it away.

- To conserve gray-water holding tank space, use dishpans to wash and rinse dishes. When finished, pour water down toilet into the black-water holding tank.

- Fabric softener sheets placed in drawers, closets, and other strategic locations in an RV prevents musty odors and that "closed up" smell. Also, reported to be a good pest repellent.

Big Rig Truckers Offer Safe Driving Tips for RVers

A team of million mile accident-free drivers are helping to make our roads safer. America's Road Team Captains, elite professional truck drivers chosen by the American Trucking Associations (ATA), are offering advice on how to safely navigate through highway traffic and congestion.

America's Road Team Captains agree that the first step toward safe RV travel begins in the driveway.

- Do a "walk around" before leaving: Check your RV's tires, wipers and fluids. Have your radiator and cooling system serviced. You can prevent many of the problems that strand RVers on the side of the road before you leave your home.

- Plan. Before you begin your RV trip, know your exits by name and number, and watch the signs for the exit as you near it. Drivers making unexpected lane changes to exit often cause accidents.

- Use a map or program your GPS. Surprisingly, not all RVers use maps, even when driving through unfamiliar areas. Knowing the road is essential for safe driving.

- Leave early and avoid risks. Leave early so you won't be anxious about arriving late. Leave early to accommodate delays.

- Know your limitations. Don't drive when tired, upset, or physically ill.

- Think Twice about changing lanes just get around a vehicle that is traveling at a speed close to yours. Never try to gain a few seconds by attempting a risky maneuver.

- Be aware of a truck's blind spots. When sharing the road with large trucks, if you can't see the truck driver in his or her mirrors, then the truck driver can't see you.

- Expect the unexpected. Look a quarter mile ahead for a safe path. Leave yourself an out.

- Signal your intentions. To change lanes, signal ahead of time so other drivers can respond. If a truck is signaling to change lanes, allow it space to do so. Often, it is trying to avoid another vehicle.

- Do not cut in front of other vehicles, especially large trucks. Remember that trucks take longer to make a complete stop, so avoid cutting quickly in front of them.

- Yield on entrance ramps. Highway traffic has the right of way. Maintain proper speed, use smooth merging techniques, and don't slow down in front of a truck.

- Never stop on the highway. The most dangerous speed on a highway is zero. Stopping your RV, even on the shoulder, can create a severe hazard for you and others. If you are stopped for emergency purposes, understand that big trucks cannot always stop to assist you, but most will use their radios to contact the police or highway patrol if they see you are in trouble.

- Stay alert in construction zones. Traffic may move more slowly, and lanes may be temporarily closed. Obey informational signs located within the work zone. Many states double fines when infractions of the law are made in construction zones.

- The America's Road Team would like to remind RVers that from driveway to highway, RV driving safety requires patience and dedication.

- ATA's America's Road Team is sponsored by Volvo Trucks North America.

http://www.trucking.org/Programs/RoadTeam/Pages/Default.aspx

RV Quick Tips

✱ Have an RV with in-floor heating vents? Get a couple of feet of fiberglass window screen fabric and put a piece under each of the vents to catch the dropped stuff, along with dirt and leaves that get tracked in. Remove the vents, lay the screen fabric down, replace the vents and trim the excess screening. Just vacuum to clean the screen.

✱ When you eat a sandwich, hamburger or hot dog, do you end up wearing most of it … ketchup, mustard, relish? Before you dig in, slide the sandwich partly into a plastic sandwich bag and the juices will drop into the bag and not on your clothes.

RV Lifestyle Tips

Save money on camping expenses

Guest writer Jaimie Hall Bruzenak offers ten ways to save money on campground expenses:

- Use a campground directory. You can cut driving miles from your route and pick out lower priced places to stay. Call ahead to verify rates and availability.

- Join a membership park or join a half-price camping club. Both offer lower rates to members. Investigate membership parks before joining. They may or may not save you money. The half-price clubs cost around $50/year for a membership that entitles you varying discounts so if you stay in three or four parks at discounted prices, you'll be ahead of the game.

- Extend your stay. Many parks offer weekly and monthly rates that lower your nightly rate.

- Try boondocking. When you are traveling and are only stopping for the night and not needing or using campground facilities, find a boondocking spot. Many RVers blacktop boondock at WalMart parking lots or at truck stops. (Be sure to follow proper etiquette.)

- Choose cheaper sites. If you don't need to dump your tanks, request a site that has only water and electric for a cheaper rate than a full-hookup site.

- Set up your rig for boondocking. Add solar panels and a catalytic or ceramic heater to your RV so you can boondock for extended periods of time on public land. There is an initial setup cost but camping is free or low-cost.

- Look for free camping. Some towns, particularly Midwestern ones, have municipal RV parks where you can stay free for a night or two.

- Stay in public campgrounds. Many public campgrounds operated by federal and state agencies are less expensive than private facilities. Many will not have hookups but are in beautiful locations.

- Stay with friends or fellow club members. Several RV clubs have lists of members who welcome club members to stop overnight for one night on their travels. If you stay with a friend or club member, don't abuse your privilege. Offer some money or take them to dinner.

- Work or volunteer where you get a free site. Many volunteer or work camper jobs come with a free or reduced-rate RV site.

Jaimie Hall Bruzenak is an RV Lifestyle Expert. She has been RVing since 1992. She and her late husband weren't retired so RVed on a budget and worked on the road. She is the author of "Support Your RV Lifestyle! An Insider's Guide to Working on the Road" and other RV books.

See http://www.RVLifestyleExperts.com for more information about the RV lifestyle.

More Ways to Extend Your RV travel Dollars

These days everyone, including RVers look for ways to save money. We've covered RV club, camping club, gas card and other discounts of interest to RVers. Here are a few more ways to extend your RV travel dollars.

Chamber of Commerce

If you're planning your trip, check out the Chamber of Commerce website for the towns and cities you plan to visit. Call or email to request an information packet by mail. If you are on the road just stop in.

Not only will these info packets have plenty of brochures and information on various local attractions, they often include discount coupons.

Dining Out

Restaurant.com is a service that sells restaurant gift vouchers at a discount. You can typically get a $25 dining certificate for less than $10. Search their database for restaurants in the areas you'll be visiting. Be sure you take advantage of Senior discounts and Senior menus.

Museums

Most major museums in the United States have one day a month or week where tickets are discounted or free. When you're doing your research and planning your outings, make sure you investigate.

Theater, Concert, Sports & Events

If you're headed to a big city and want to take in a show, concert, ball game or other event look for a discount ticket outlet. They sell off unsold event seats at the last minute at considerable discounts. Here are a couple sites to check out: Goldstar.com and Stubhub.com

American Automobile Association

If you belong to AAA, ask about them about discounts on hotel, restaurant, theme park and other offers along your route.

Getting Medical Prescriptions While Full-time RVing

I have always used Walgreens for prescriptions, even after we began full time RVing. I have an online account with them and can order, name the time I will pick them up and the location. Most large population areas have Walgreens. In our loop through the U.S. one summer from Yuba City, California to Lockport, New York and back by a different route I had no difficulty finding a Walgreens from the list of stores on their website.

Also, if you are not going to be near one, or just don't want to go to one they will ship your RX to you. They also handle contacting your physician when a prescription needs to be renewed.

Many other pharmacies offer the same service... WalMart, for one, may of interest to RVers. -- *Fran*

Grab and Go Bag

Almost every RVer either has a vehicle that tows the RV or an RV that tows a vehicle for exploring while the RV is parked somewhere. In either instance the RVer(s) move back and forth from the RV to the vehicle quite frequently taking with them certain wants and needs of their daily lives. Other items in this category are often purchased in duplicate so that when needed one would be found stored in the RV and another would be stashed in the tow or 'toad' vehicle.

Instead of having two of each of some of these items why not fix a 'go bag' that holds the stuff you need and you can just grab it on your way out the door. First aid supplies, water, sun visor, sun glasses, gum, snacks or a picnic, sun block, extra set of ear buds, small pack of handy (baby) wipes, save space for a small camera and maybe your laptop, a map of the surrounding area, pencil or pen and notepad…you know what you'll want for each trip and if your go-bag is always handy you can toss in items as you prepare to depart for any occasion.

A roomy canvas bag with easy to grab strap handles is a great thing. Mine will sit and stay open so I can pop stuff into it easily. It has a row of pockets around the outside that can hold small stuff. It is a sort of carpenter's tool bag that I once used to hold my woodcarving tools until I got so many I needed a regular toolbox for them all.

Natural Disaster Tips for Rvers

There are times when no amount of readiness can solve problems created by natural disasters but that doesn't mean you shouldn't try to be prepared. Storage space in your RV and the distance of your location from your family and friends may be special considerations for RVers, especially full timers.

Some things you can do to be prepared, some of which may already be part of your camping and traveling lifestyle.

- Have a two to three day supply of water about a gallon or more per person per day… for drinking, cooking, washing hands. Your fresh water tank could contain additional water.

- Check your First Aid kits to replenish used items and check other items to determine their freshness.

- Make sure flashlights are handy and functional. Have extra bulbs of the types your flashlights use.

- Keep a supply of batteries of sizes you need for flashlight, radios, the battery operated can opener (smile), etc.

- Make sure you have a working, battery powered radio.

- A set of two-way hand-held radios with good batteries.

- Paper maps in case your GPS doesn't function.

- A generator and fuel would be nice also.

How 'bout a positive attitude because once a disaster happens you can not make it back as it was. The only way to go is forward and, as Theodore Roosevelt said: "Do what you can, with what you have, where you are."

What RVers Should Do When Tornados Threaten

You are traveling in 'tornado alley' or any other location known to be subject to tornadoes. The sky is increasingly dark, gray, threatening ...the wind is picking up. It's time to turn off the CD music and turn on NOAA or connect with a local radio station.

NOAA Weather Radio All Hazards broadcasts are available online as live streaming audio. These streams are hosted by third parties such as universities ...and listings are grouped by state.

If you are on the road you should know where you are ...that is, the highway you are on and a town or city you are near. You should also know the township, county and state you are in if you are parked, and where you are headed from that position.

Urban areas have alert systems. Warning signals may differ in different locations. If you are parked the RV Park manager should be able to tell you what to listen for. If not, contact the local police department (on a non-emergency line).

TORNADO WATCH: The early alert means tornadoes are possible where you are located. Remain aware of approaching storms. Local radio and television stations will broadcast the alert. Stay informed. In a RV park ask the manager the best place to be and if and when you must abandon your recreational vehicle.

TORNADO WARNING: A tornado has been sighted or indicated by weather radar. If a tornado warning is issued for your area and the sky becomes threatening, move to your pre-designated place of safety. The Fire Department will sound alarms.

The sound of a tornado is classically described as being similar to that of a speeding freight train rumbling in the distance and may be heard but not seen after dark. In daylight keep alert and continually monitor the sky around you.

Environmental clues to watch for:

- Dark, often greenish sky

- Turbulent, swirling clouds

- Large hail

- Loud roar; similar to a freight train

Caution: Some tornadoes appear as a visible funnel extending only partially from a cloud. Likely, below the visible funnel, there is a column of rotating air that cannot be seen until it begins to pick up dirt and debris as it moves along and touches down. Funnel clouds can look to be narrow at first, when they drop from the clouds. Ones that have touched down and are moving along the surface in your direction look like a huge, ground to cloud, dark wall.

Make the decision!

Every year, many folks are killed or seriously injured by tornados despite advanced warning.

Being prepared and staying up to date with timely severe weather watches and warnings, could save your life in the event a tornado threatens where you are. After you have received the warning or observed threatening skies, YOU must make the decision to seek shelter before the storm arrives. It could be the most important decision you will ever make.

As some point you must realize that you can probably do nothing to save your RV and other possessions. Make a decision to do everything you can to save your people and your pets. Get them into a ditch ...below ground level if possible ...a stairwell, concrete basement.

Personal Property Insurance for RVers

Base coverage for personal property in most RV Insurance policies is inadequate. That's especially true for full time RVers but even weekend and vacation RVers can load many expensive things into an RV. Take some time to inventory everything, and do your best to set a replacement value for each item.

You may be surprised to find the replacement cost of high-value items such as LCD TVs, satellite TV and internet systems, computers and peripherals, cameras, GPs units, antiques, firearms, jewelry, musical instruments and collections are worth much more than the base coverage. If so, you should buy additional scheduled personal property coverage.

Start outside your RV and record everything kept in outside storage compartments. Once inside, work from front to back so you don't overlook anything.

Open drawers, cupboards, closets, storage bins and toolboxes and record their contents. Don't forget any special furniture, appliances, or decorations you've added to your rig.

One RVer suggested using your digital camera to record everything of value in your RV. Reduce the file size of the photos to about 35~40 KB then upload them to an online storage account like G-mail, or a photo album like Shutterfly.com or Flickr.com. Just remember to set the album to private. Then should the worst happen, you will have visual proof of what you owned. Insurance companies won't pay for anything that you can't prove you possessed.

Tips for Getting Your Mail on the Road

Finding a satisfactory way to get your mail while RVing may be perplexing at first but it can be worked out in a way that suits your RV lifestyle. Here are some things to consider:

- If you make short trips in your RV and return to a house without wheels (HWW) 'back home' you might be able to let the mail be delivered as usual to your home and have a friend or neighbor collect it, package it and then send it to you. Depending on how long your trips are and how many trips you take, having a friend or relative pick up the mail from your home or P.O.Box and hold it until you send for it may put a strain on your helper's busy life.

- Clubs like the Escapees RV Club and Family Motor Coach Association offer mail forwarding for their members although their services are better suited to full time RVers. Most club members who use the services are very happy with them.

- Check the Escapee Club Website for their Mail Service information. They personalize your service to fit your every need. If you are full time, your permanent address can be in Livingston, Texas, the home of the Escapee Club, and your mail will be forwarded to you when and where you request it. Only problem may be when you stop or base out of somewhere else for longer periods of time you still have a short wait to get your mail.

- The Family Motor Coach Association Mailing Service is for FMCA members. You must own a motor home to be a member of FMCA.

- There are other options. Contract with a commercial mail forwarding service in your home base area. They seem to be blooming almost everywhere. Some are franchises, some are connected with delivery services (UPS, FedEx, etc.) and some are mom-pop type businesses combined with gift shops, book stores, packaging/shipping stores, etc. You can use their street address for your permanent address and rent a box, called a Personal Mail Box (PMB, is NOT a post office box) and perhaps a suite number or letter if it is located in a strip mall.

- All mail forwarding services operate pretty much the same, it's the details that separate out the good ones. Go beyond the basics and price when asking questions. Some things to consider are: How long has the service been in business. Does the company look prosperous. You will have to change your address if the company goes out of business.

- What is the best way to communicate with the service? Use their 800 phone number if they have one, use their regular business number if not, email, or USPS?

- Hours. When can you call, anytime during business hours or specific times?

- How soon will they forward your mail once you call? A prompt mailing means you won't have to wait long for your mail.

Tips for Staying Warm in Your RV

Here's a few tips to ensure you have a warm and pleasurable cold-weather RV camping experience.

- Typical RV windows don't keep the heat in very well. A Window Insulator Kit provides a layer of insulation film without obstructing the view. The easy-to-install kit requires only scissors and a hair dryer for installation. Safe for application to aluminum, painted or varnished wood, or vinyl clad window moulding. Film wrinkles are removed with a hair dryer. Double stick tape is included.

- Make sure all furnace vents are open and unobstructed.

- Ceramic space heaters are very effective for heating RVs and cost much less than running your furnace. For safety, make sure that your heater has a tip-over switch and remember to unplug it when you leave your RV.

- Consider installing a catalytic heater. They are very safe if used according to manufacturer instructions. They use propane very efficiently.

- Roof vents let much heat escape. There are foam type pillows specifically made to fit snugly in vent openings and greatly reduce heat loss.

- If your RV has a ceiling fan use it to circulate the warmer air that collects at the ceiling.

- If you have a motorhome, hang a heavy blanket or privacy curtain between the driver's compartment and the rest of the coach to block the cold radiated by the windshield.

- Heavier clothes will help you stay warm in cold weather. Wear a sweater or sweatshirt.

- Keep a throw blanket handy to cover your legs and feet or shoulders. Fleece blankets and throws are particularly useful, because they are warm but lightweight.

- Keep your socks and shoes on or wear slippers in your RV. Much body heat is lost through bare feet.

- Try a heating pad temporarily for warmth. If you use a heating pad for warmth, limit the time it's close to the skin to avoid a burn.

RV Quick Tip

✱ To remove the soap and hard water build-up on shower walls and doors use straight white vinegar. Use a spray bottle to spray the white vinegar straight onto the surface and let set for a minimum of ten minutes then rinse. On stubborn build up wipe with a damp cloth sprinkled with some baking soda. In tighter areas, apply vinegar and scrub with a toothbrush dipped in baking soda.

Tips On Packing Your RV for Vacation

- Before you start packing, unpack. Use the opportunity to clean the interior including closets, cupboards, and pantry and take everything out of the RV that won't be needed on the trip. Don't forget the outside storages compartments.

- Pack backward. What you load first in the RV should be what you will use last or least. So you can get to them easily, things you'll need while en route, like snacks, games, maps and other trip aids should get packed last.

- Snacks for the road. Munching is a typical activity on RV road trips, but try to keep it healthy! Before you leave on a camping trip, set out bowls of raisins, granola and various nuts and let each person fill a bag.

- Watch your weight. Be aware of your GVWR (Gross Vehicle Weight Rating), your GVCR (Gross Vehicle Combination Rating), NCC (Net Carrying Capacity) etc. Realize that what your unit can carry is limited.

Ten Steps to a Full Time RVing Lifestyle

1. Have a partner that you get along with ... well. That is love, care about their well-being, enjoy mutual activities and can tolerate their idiosyncrasies.

2. Join the Escapees Club, or club(s) of your choice, and/or an online forum to get a feel for what it's all about.

3. Decide how much you want to be on the road versus how much you want to spend a couple weeks or months in one place.

4. Find the RV you like and think you can spend good times in.

5. Try a couple weeks, then a month or so of living/traveling/camping in your RV before you sell your stick house and dump your lifetime accumulation of possessions.

If you get through the first five steps successfully it's time to get serious.

6. Find a place for your 'base' … a town with relatives/friends/ health care connections, etc..

7. Choose a mail service to receive all your mail, including packages, and hold it for you, then forward it on as directed by you when you have an address. Friends/relatives may offer but a service.

8. Choose a cellular phone service. Disconnect your landline service. Make sure your computer is updated and has WiFi.

9. Sort and eliminate stuff you have collected over the years. At least 75% of it. Do NOT rent a storage unit …after a year or so you won't even remember what's in it. If you want to remember some stuff… photograph it and put it on the screen saver or roll-over of your computer.

10. Have an estate sale. donate what isn't sold to a charity thrift store. Sell your stick house.

11. Tell your friends and relatives that you love them, you will miss them, you will communicate by phone, computer, skype or snail mail. Tell them you will send them photos and travel logs about the good times you are having and things you are seeing. Ask them to please step back because you'd hate to run over their feet with your RV. Then head on down the road to the freedom of a new-to-you lifestyle.

Special Insurance for Full Time RVers

Typical RV insurance policies are not written with the full time RVer in mind. However, there are special policies just for full time RVers that cover contingencies usually covered by one's homeowner policy.

If you are a full time RVer you do not have a homeowner policy to fall back on so you will certainly want to have a good property damage rider on your RV insurance policy. Since full time Rvers usually carry more stuff it's even more important to know the limit of the property damage rider compared to the value of the personal property aboard the RV.

The amount of personal property damage coverage in an RV insurance policy is very small and may not cover all of your valuables and other possessions in the case of a major accident. Especially in today's modern RVs with computers, large TVs etc. Don't forget to include in your estimate of value for things such as hobby tools you my have aboard …golf equipment, wood carving tools, metal detectors, photography equipment, musical instruments, fishing poles, tennis rackets, lawn furniture, barbecues …it all adds up when you need to replace it.

If you carry many expensive things with you as you travel, you may need to increase your personal property insurance coverage to an amount that will replace them should they be destroyed. Often times increasing this kind of coverage is not very expensive, so check to see what is offered.

As with any personal property insurance, a well documented inventory of your possessions is the only way to get fully compensated for any losses when you make a claim.

Choosing Your Home State as a Full Time RVer

by Fran Crawford

RVers who have spent weekends, weeks, and/or months vacationing in RVs while raising families and working at careers often look forward to a day when they can 'hit the road' full time. Planning for such a lifestyle change can be fun as well as educational.

One of the first things that needs to be decided to get away on your new adventure is what state would be best for your home base. It could be the state where you are living when you decide to retire. Will you still own property there? It could be a state you have visited and loved enough to want to call it home.

Many states require that you own or rent a home to claim residency and vote.

A home base where you don't own property could be a state where you have family or close friends that draw you there to visit occasionally. It could be a place where you would want to visit for medical or dental checkups or procedures and where you might do your banking, register your vehicles and operators licenses. Regulation varies by state so be sure to check about having your rig registered where you are domiciled.

State income tax is another facet to be recognized and handled. You can find a chart of state tax rates and those states that have none at this web address: http://www.taxadmin.org/fta/rate/ind_inc.html

Texas is one of the states with no income tax. The Escapees RV club is in Livingston, Texas, and can handle mailing and other services for RVers. Find more about them, what membership in the Escapees will do for you, and how to join the club at: http://www.escapees.com

There are other options for handling your mail in most cities of any size at all. The USPS does not do 'holding' or 'forwarding' services so a post office box is not the best way to go.

There is, of course, the option of having your mail sent to a relative or good friend but it but it can become quite a burden for someone to handle the forwarding of it all to you.

A mailing service can rent you a PMB (Personal Mail Box) and a Suite ID as well as a street (physical) address for a place to have your mail sent. They will receive packages for you from any delivery service and hold, or forward stuff to addresses you provide for them by phone or email.

Internet Access on the Road with WiFi

WiFi may be the most popular method RVers use to get internet access while traveling.

WiFi stands for Wireless Fidelity. It's also know as 802.11 and Macintosh computer users call it AirPort. Whatever you call it, WiFi is a basic two-way radio with about a 300 foot range and software that sends and receives standard internet data.

Manufacturers have been building WiFi technology in to laptops for several years. I doubt there is a now laptop that doesn't have WiFi. It's just a matter of learning how to use it and it's easier than you think.

Places where internet access is provided by WiFi are often called hotspots and hotspots are available in restaurants, coffee shops, convenience stores, hotels, motels, airports, truck stops and RV parks and campgrounds. Just about anyplace where people congregate is likely to have a hotspot in the next few years.

While many hotspots are pay-for-service, the trend is toward providing free service. RV parks generally offer free WiFi as an amenity while truck stops usually charge.

Truck stops and other locations that charge a fee usually have pay-as-you-go plans as well as subscription plans. If you travel a lot and frequent the same chain for fuel stops a subscription could be cost effective.

There is more than one WiFi standard…the old 'b', the 'g' standard which is still in wide use and "N" the current standard.

The 'g' standard offers better security and faster speed over the 'b' and likewise 'n' is a speed and security improvement over 'g'. Don't let the different standards bother you too much though. Most hotspots will accept all WiFi standards for the foreseeable future.

I will add here that on our recent cross country trip we had fair luck finding WiFi at the parks we stayed in. Most had WiFi but the service varied from unusable to excellent. Ironically the excellent WiFi was in a somewhat rundown RV park with no other amenities. At $17 a night it was one of the least expensive too although we did pay $3 for the WiFi. Still cheap!

WiFi service is widely available and usually free so any RVer who wants to have internet access should have WiFi capability.

Tips for Using WiFi at RV Parks and Other Places

Even though WiFi isn't everywhere there are enough hotspots (locations with a WiFi internet access point) in places RVers go to make it worthwhile to use it.

Certainly fee-based hotspots will be around for the next few years but it seems WiFi is becoming just another free amenity.

Free hotspots are also offered by other retail businesses that feel the service sets them apart from their competition and attracts customers.

Even Starbucks now provides free WiFi if you're willing to buy a cup of coffee. If you are an AT&T DSL subscriber you don't even have to  buy the coffee… but you should anyway. Panera Bread Cafes, McDonalds, are just some of the places you can find free WiFi.

Wi-Fi is also frequently offered by public agencies… libraries, schools, public parks, etc. In many areas. WiFi users themselves are working together to provide free hotspots to the community.

Of special interest to RVers are the many RV parks which are installing Wi-Fi as a guest amenity. As with other hotspots some parks have a charge and others offer Wi-Fi for free.

Some RV parks are installing Wi-Fi access points in their activity centers and other common areas but others are covering the entire park so that guests can have access at their site.

You only need to know the SSID (service set identifier) for the park's network and your computer with installed Wi-Fi will be able to join the park's wireless network. Your Wi-Fi utility will tell if an Access Point is in range and what it's SSID is.

You should be able to join the network without problems. If the service is free then your good to start surfing and downloading your email.

If the RV park charges a fee to use the WiFi you'll know when you try to surf the net with your browser. Fee based hotspots usually use a Captive Portal which simply means that you will only be able to see the hotspot provider's web page which will offer a way to pay for internet access. Just follow the instructions on the web page to make your payment and get online.

There are two major hotspot service providers that specialize in providing fee-based WiFi internet to RV parks, Tengo Internet and LinkSpot. Each has a directory of the parks they service.

RV Quick Tip

✱   When parking at a curb that the top of the vehicle may be hanging over the curb due to slope of the street. It's easy to hit a light pole, or tree that's too close to the street.

5 Ways to protect your information when using WiFi Hotspots

RVers often look for and use public WiFi hotspots at RV parks, travel plazas and rest areas. Public hotspots are open and unencrypted so by nature are insecure. Information you transmit through your laptop or smartphone, may very well fall into the wrong hands. There are ways to stay safe, however. They are:

- Set your Wi-Fi device to disallow automatic connection to opens networks. By doing so, you will always know when you're connecting to an open Wi-Fi hotspot. Auto-configuration is most popular on smart phones but many laptops are configured that way by default.

- When using a public hotspot make sure you disable sharing. If there's a storage device or other computers on your home network, you may have sharing enabled on your laptop.

- If you're conducting business or sharing sensitive information, it's best to use a virtual private network (VPN), which creates an encrypted, private link across a public network.

- Use a personal firewall, either the one that came with your Mac or Windows PC, or a third-party app from a reputable security vendor. Firewalls come with a range of configurations. At a minimum, you will want to know when another computer is attempting to gain access to your system.

- When paying bills and shopping online using a hotspot, it's best if the hotspot has WPA2 security. At the least make sure the website has a secure connection. A site is securer if there is an 'https' in your browser's web address bar.

Internet Access on the Road with Cellular Data Devices

If you are an RVer who needs reliable internet access you should probably have a cellular data plan.

There are two types of cellular data devices: WiFi hotspots and USB modems. USB modems are still in use but WiFi hotspot devices, such as the one pictured here, are popular among many RVers.

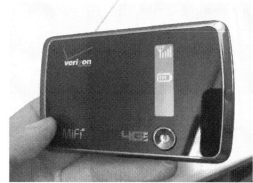

The top cellular providers usually require a separate 'data plan' and all have about the same pricing …about $60/month. Although what you get for your money varies between providers.

The service is easy to set up and use. If you can get a cell signal, you usually can get online. The 3G service speed is about the same as DSL but can be as slow as 2x dial up speed in remote areas.

Cellular data service is still mostly 3G especially in the rural areas where RVers typically hang out but 4G service is building out and it is much faster. If you are buying a new cellular data device you should consider getting one that is 4G capable so you'll be ready wherever it is available. Just know that you will mostly be stuck wit 3G service.

Smart phone with internet capabilities

The internet experience is limited by the small screen size. A smart phone is most useful for casual email and web browsing. The phones are pricey and service plans often cost as much or more than a typical data plan.

These are practical only for RVers who take short trips...
weekends or vacations... and only require casual internet access.

Satellite Internet Service for RVers

Back a few years ago,
before cellular data service
was available outside the
cities and few RV parks
offed WiFi, satellite
internet was big with
RVers. Fran and I used it
for little over a year around
2006 and we were happy
to have it despite the
aggravations. Today, you
won't see too many RVers
using it. In fact, I have not
seen one for a long time.

I actually debated
leaving this tip in the book
but RVers still ask about it so I left it in.

Satellite Internet is practical only to RVers who absolutely need
internet access wherever they park. It should be a last resort for
other RVers simply because of the less expensive and more
convenient options outlined previously.

There are still RVers using both Automatic and manual satellite
systems but the reality is that as cellular data coverage increases,
more Rvers abandon satellite internet.

The cost of service is about the same as cellular data plans with
similar service speeds. However latency...the time it takes for the
signal to go up to the satellite and back down...adds a noticeable
delay to webpage loading and email downloads.

To be usable the satellite dish needs an open view of the southern sky.

Manual set-up equipment starts at about $1300 and finding room to store the tripod and dish while traveling can be a problem.

Roof-mounted automatic systems (that find the satellite for you) start at about $4000. As with roof top TV satellite dishes, parking may be tricky at places with trees or hills that may block the southern sky view.

RV Quick Tips

✱ When you have to work outside in the cold at a task that requites some finger dexterity, gloves won't always work for you. In that case, try surgical gloves like we wear when dealing with the black tank. They will keep the hands a little warmer than going bear handed, but still leave your hands free to work. Put them on in layers if needed.

✱ To keep items from rattling and shifting out of place while you drive, buy a small bag of toy balloons. Blow them up about three quarters full and pinch them in between stacked plates and the shelf above. They provide a nice flexible cushion. Use different size balloons for different sizes and shapes, as needed.

✱ In bad weather, the power cord and water hose can get pretty muddy and stowing them away when breaking camp can get be a dirty job. A good terrycloth rag helps when coiling them for storage but you may want to consider using an oven mitt or car polishing mitt instead.

✱ If you use your RV much you no doubt visit a laundromat from time to time. Many lists of tips suggest 35mm film canisters make good storage containers for quarters. But these days film canisters are harder to find than film cameras. We've been using the flip-top tubes from mini M&M candies. Buy the large size tube, enjoy the candy, and you can collect enough quarters for the biggest laundry day.

Tips for Work Campers

Earning a Living While Full Time RVing

Earning a living while full time RVing depends a lot on your lifestyle and how much money you need to get along if you have some pension, have a lot of bills etc. There are as many ways working while RVing as there are full time RVers and as many ways to work while full timing as there are full timers who work. Everyone's health and abilities and interests are unique and that's what determines the kind of work they do.

To get an idea of the jobs available for RVers visit Workamper News http://www.workamper.com and Work For RVers and Campers http://www.work-for-rvers-and-campers.com. You will find listings for jobs at both sites. Most of these jobs are in campgrounds and RV parks as managers, maintenance, registration, bathroom cleaning, mini-mart, and grounds keeping. But other kinds of jobs are also listed. Also check out the Coolworks http://coolworks.com web site. It's not specifically for RVers but does have jobs for and of interest to RVers.

Advice for RVers Considering Work Camping

RVer and work camper David Carter offers these Tips

We find work camping VERY beneficial for us and the Campground owners. We have made some lasting friendships with the people we have met while we work camped.

As for our benefits we are able to stay in an area we choose to explore extensively at a very reasonable cost or even no expense to us. If there is an area we are interested in, we pick a city or location centrally located so that all we want to explore is just a short drive in our toad. For longer drives we usually book a cheap hotel room and spend a night or two. It's actually cheaper and easier than unhooking and moving our "Tin-can-dominium." Additionally there is no space rent to pay when you leave your RV parked where you work camp. The hotel stays are a nice change too. It can be a romantic get away, especially if you splurge to get a spa tub in the room!

Another advantage of work camping in an area you want to explore is you have the time to leisurely experience the locals and get to know "their way of life and viewpoints". We like to locate the locals favorite eatery, frequent it regularly and within the first week or two develop some valuable friendships.

We have been invited to go fishing, hunting, bowling, horseback riding, to county fairs, museum functions, para-sailing, to their lake cottages, cocktail parties, family BBQs, nature hikes, you name it. Our list is endless of what we have been invited to do and have done, that only the locals know about.

Advice for Novice Work Campers

David Carter continues with these Tips:

I have told many new work campers that campground owners will ask for and want everything possible from a work camper candidate, that's understandable when you are in their shoes. It's the ask for the world and see what you end up with theory.

Most will fit you into their job openings if you are honest & frank when you let them know your skills and the accurate times you are available.

From our experience work camping, we have found the campground owners would "prefer" a office person familiar with their front office "F/O" registration software programs. Training time and supervision greatly reduces the time before a new work camper can work independently. As the work camper becomes proficient with the F/O system, the usual 3 month commitment is over and the campground owner has to start all over from the beginning with a new work camper.

I have found that if you really want to work camp in a specific location and the job posting is a "must have experience" type, you should emphasize to the campground owner you are a quick learner, you would really like to learn the program to better yourself for future work camper gigs and would commit to at least 6 months at their campground. We have learned most all campground F/O programs this way. Trust me, they are not that difficult to master and all are really quite similar. You just have to memorize the key stroke steps and where to find certain info.

Another idea some fellow work campers have told me that has worked well for them is they will "moonlight" at another CG (Other that the one they are work camping at) in their reservation office on a phone desk & learn that way. There is no direct customer contact like at the check in counter so it is much quicker and easier to learn the program without the guest questions & interruptions.

When campground owners tell me all their positions are filled I let them know that from my previous experiences some work campers just don't work out, please keep us in mind, and when we do arrive in their area as planned we will drop by & introduce ourselves. We have landed great work camper gigs that way too. The CG owner now has a "Plan B" to cover any positions of the work campers that are just not fitting in. There is usually 1 in every work camping group.

More Advice for New Work Campers

Vicki Yasment offers her advice for new work campers.

I am doing the campground host/workcamper thing here at Lazy Acres Campground in Elberta, AL.

The way I started work camping was through the Florida State parks system. I used to volunteer as campground host selling ice and firewood, answering visitor questions and yup, cleaning the bath houses. Might be a good way for others to get some experience to move up to other campground positions.

I know some parks already have snowbirds in place that return year after year and, some even have waiting lists. Set your starting point low, the larger the park, the more experience they may require. Also, don't limit yourself to office/check-in station work. Start by working out in the park and maybe you can work your way to your desired office job once they get to know you and trust your work abilities.

When I came to my present park which, is a small campground, owned by a wife and husband, I had no intention on becoming the host in the campground, activities director and, check-in/office girl two days a week. I got to know the owners very well. They liked me and, from our conversations, they knew I had done camp hosting before. I happened to mention things I had done in the past, some ideas of which I had learned from other places I had camped (my secret) and the owners recognized that I had experience.

This park had no activities or camp store when I came here. We have both now. I just kept "nudging" her to let me at least start having bingo. Once she saw me in action and, could trust me to do a good job, it opened other possibilities for me. I had no previous check in station experience but, one day she asked me if I was interested in a job so here I am now.

I believe the more you give the more you get. I am only required to work two days a week in the office from 9:30 am to 5 pm. Many days, I end up getting out later. If I know I have a late arrival on the way, and they are close by, I will stay late to wait for them.

It was my idea to start up the activities (we have activities year round, most campgrounds only during the season). As campground host on Sundays when the office/store is closed, campers know they can come to my door and I will open the store to sell them whatever they need. My phone number is on the answering machine for after hours help.

My latest venture was to get wifi for the park. I found a company that will do it with nothing out of our pocket and, we do nothing but sit back and collect our percentage of the monies that it generates.

All that was on my time by my choice to better the campground. The owners appreciate that and give my ideas serious consideration since I have done nothing but help the revenue.

I feel that if a small campground has the abilities and manpower to improve then, the owners should consider ideas from full time campers. We have been around and, seen things that work, things that campers desire and we are full of ideas. I was lucky enough to stumble upon such a place and, we are getting busier every day as word of mouth spreads.

I am now "nudging" to become campground manager since both owners work full time. Only time will tell but, we have been here over a year now and I still love the place. — Vicki

Working RVer Tips

Today's tip is provided by Coleen Sykora editor of Work for RVers and Campers http://www.work-for-rvers-and-campers.com.

Yes, it is possible – and practical – to make enough money to live in an RV full-time, travel, and enjoy life! There are more jobs for RVers and work campers than there are RVers and campers willing to work. You can also earn a living running a business from your RV. Here's a couple of tips.

Increase Your Compensation with Additional Benefits

If you can't negotiate higher wages with an employer, you might ask for one or more other benefits, such as these:

- Meals and beverages

- Ice or freezer space

- College classes

- Rafting, kayaking, or sight-seeing trips

- Use of laundry facilities

- Use of company car

- Propane

- Passes to attractions and events

- Guided tours and excursions

- Store discounts

- Off season housing or RV storage

- An RV site for a visiting friend for a couple days

- Use of company tools, boats, bicycles, or other equipment

Ways RVers Make Money

- Flight seeing guide

- Building construction work

- Sell cookware at home and RV shows

- Water park attendant

- Service portable toilets

- Campground grounds keeper

- Teach aerobics - Visit Coleen's website for more information about working RVers.

RV Quick Tips

✱ When you have to work outside in the cold at a task that requites some finger dexterity, gloves won't always work for you. In that case, try surgical gloves like we wear when dealing with the black tank. They will keep the hands a little warmer than going bear handed, but still leave your hands free to work. Put them on in layers if needed.

✱ Never dump the black tank unless it's at least 2/3rds full. If you want to dump it sooner then add water to the tank.

✱ After dumping, rinse the tank with either a toilet rinse wand or the built-in rinsing system if you have one. When the tank is flushed 'clean' close the valve and add enough water to cover the bottom of the tank.

✱ When using the toilet use plenty of water when flushing... at least until the tank is about 1/4 full.

✱ Most every RV has a gravity fill port for the fresh water tank. You just stick the end of a hose in the port and let it run till the tank is full.

✱ During the summer... when you're not using the furnace ... cover floor vents with with a sheet of magnetized vinyl cut to size. The material is available at craft stores and sign shops and can be spray painted a color to match the interior of your rig.

✱ Our fifth wheel has two entry doors with separate keys. To tell the difference I just removed the plastic cap from the rear door key. The plastic cap on the front door key... the one we use most... makes it easier to find on my key ring. The rear door key is on the same ring next to the front door key so it's easy to find too.

RV Battery Tips

12-volt RV Battery Basics

A 12-volt battery is not really a 12-volt battery. It's just a convenient term. A fully-charged 12-volt battery in good condition, allowed to "rest" for a few hours (or days) with no load being drawn from it or charge going to it, will balance out its charge and measure about 12.6 volts between terminals.

When a battery reads only 12 volts under the above conditions, it's almost fully depleted. Actually, if a battery's resting voltage … after charging… is only 12.0 to 12.1 it means only 20 to 25% of its useful energy remains and it probably needs to be replaced.

12-volt batteries supply useful energy only through a limited range — from over 14 volts (when fully charged and unrested) down to 10.5 volts in use under load (when lights dim, pumps groan and TV pictures get small).

No 12-volt battery will remain at over 14 volts for more than seconds unless it's being charged. The lowest limit is 10.5 volts but this is too low and unsatisfactory in practical use.

Experienced RVers try to use no more than 20% to 50% of the energy available in a battery before recharging. That means they never let resting voltage get below 12.5. They never use more than 50% before recharging (resting volts of 12.3) except in an emergency. They know that, if resting voltage ever reaches 12.1, they have deep-discharged one cycle and that a battery is good for only so many cycles (from as low as 20 in an automotive battery to 180 in a golf cart battery, with the typical RV/marine battery good for no more than 30).

Chassis & House Battery Differences

There are battery types for different purposes. It's important know the difference because the chassis battery and the 'coach' or house battery are different types.

A chassis battery starts the engine and runs the automotive systems in a motor home or the tow vehicle. A coach battery powers the lights, furnace, water pump and other 12 volt devices in the coach.

The chassis or engine starting battery is constructed of many thin plates to supply high current for the short time it takes to start a cold engine. It is then quickly recharged by the engine alternator.

A deep cycle RV battery for the coach or trailer is built with fewer but thick lead plates to supply relatively smaller amounts of current for long periods of time without needing to be recharged right away. A deep cycle battery requires a longer recharge time at a lower current level to be fully and safely recharged. The properties of the deep cycle battery make it ideal for use as an RV house battery.

CCA (Cold Cranking Amps)

A test conducted at 0°F measures the maximum current a battery will produce, for only 30 seconds, down to an end voltage of only 7.2V. (Note that maximum current is never stated.) This test is valid only in selecting the battery to be used in starting your engine. It cannot be converted to a figure useful in determining low amp draw over long periods as in the RV house battery.

AH (Ampere Hour) Rating

A given number of amps for a given number of hours (amps x hours) down to an end point of 10.5V is used to calculate the frequently seen AH rating. The 10.5V end point is standard. Some manufacturers put the AH rating on their batteries ...they just don't tell you how they measured it. The retailer may provide a chart listing capacities in amps and time. Multiplying these will allow comparing one brand against another.

Lead/Acid Battery Maintenance

If your battery has removable vent caps they can be twisted open or pried off with a flat-blade screwdriver depending on the type of cap. Once removed, you will see individual fill tubes (in a 12-volt battery there are 6 of these tubes). Look down into each individual cell to make sure that the water is covering the lead plates and is at the proper level. Add distilled water to any cells that are low. Ideally, the water level should be no higher than just below, or to the bottom of, the fill tubes that go down into the battery.

Always use distilled water to fill the battery in order to prevent chemicals from contaminating the battery.

Step by Step Battery Maintenance

- Clean the exterior of the battery of corrosion and dirt.

- If the battery is not sealed, check the electrolyte level of your RV battery. Add distilled water as necessary.

- Check the cables for breaks, corrosion or stripped insulation.

- Check that the terminals are tightly fitted to the cables. Repair or replace as necessary.

- Disconnect cables from the battery, negative terminal first, and clean cables with a solution of baking soda and water.

- Scrub the terminals with a wire brush.

- Clean the battery terminal posts with the baking soda and water solution.

- Reconnect the battery cables.

- Apply a thin layer of battery post grease to the terminal posts. White lithium spray-on grease works well.

Tips & Warnings

- The most common causes of premature battery failure are overcharging, sustained undercharging, sulfation and poor maintenance.

- When charging, batteries give off explosive hydrogen gas. Avoid electrical arcing and avoid smoking or open flames.

- Electrolyte (battery acid) is corrosive to metal, skin, just about everything.

- If acid is spilled or splashed on skin flush with water to neutralize the acid, and consider medical attention.

- If acid is splashed into eyes, flush with baking soda and water to neutralize the acid, continue flushing until you get medical attention.

- Wear old clothing when working on lead/acid batteries. One unnoticed drop on clothing will discolor and even eat a hole.

- We highly recommend wearing safety glasses when working with lead/acid batteries.

RV Quick Tip

✱ Most of the outside of the RV is exposed to weather, including the A/C plugs that may be available in various compartments. I went to Home Depot and bought some male and female plug ends, such as you would use to make or repair an extension cord. I filled them with a silicon compound, to keep them water tight. When I am not using the ourdoor plugs I just stick one of these in there. It keeps the inside contacts fresh and untarnished.

RV Battery Terminal Maintenance

An RVbasics Yahoo group member reported he was having trouble with his coach battery… it wouldn't start his generator. He said the monitor panel showed the battery was charged so he couldn't figure out why the generator wouldn't start. Many members replied with helpful advice and he said he would let us know what he found.

So, what was the problem? Corrosion on the battery posts. He admitted that he had not checked for that originally because they looked clean.

Some RVers think if the battery terminal connections look clean then everything is okay. However it is the corrosion that develops between the posts and the cable clamps that needs to be checked and cleaned.

After checking that the battery is charged, cleaning the battery posts and clamps is the second thing to do whenever you are having a battery problem. Ironically, no one in the group offered that piece of advice.

To clean the battery posts and terminal clamps apply some baking soda to the posts and clamps and scrub with a wet toothbrush or similar type brush until the corrosion is gone. Clean up with dry rag. For best results use a battery terminal brush to further condition the posts and clamps. Be sure you wear old clothes… one very small drop of battery acid can make a good-sized hole or at the least bleach them.

Battery post and clamp brushes are available at your auto parts store. They are wire brushes that fit over the post and into the clamps. Even the best brushes are inexpensive so there is no excuse not to get a good quality one.

Batteries Help Make RVs Self-Contained

A big part of what makes an RV self-contained is its battery.

Some RVers say one 12 volt battery will last them about 48 hours if they don't run the furnace, carefully use the lights and water pump and otherwise conserve power. Some even use candles or go to bed early.

Once, when a storm knocked out power lines, Fran and I managed for about 15 hours in our fifth wheel with some furnace use (it was cold out) and modest use of lights. But the batteries were deeply discharged. We have two 12 volt batteries.

How long your RV battery or batteries will sustain you depends on how well you manage power usage. Try disconnecting from shore power to see how long you can go before you need to. Don't completely discharge them though, it's not good for them.

RV Battery Power Management

How long can you run lights, TV, furnace water pump etc., before battery recharging is needed? Getting the most from your batteries is a mix of conservation, intelligent charging and proper care.

Follow the steps below to determine how many days you can rally or boondock before cranking up the generator. It's best to do this test when you have an electrical hookup available so you can recharge the batteries as soon as possible.

1. Start with fully charged batteries.

2. Switch the refrigerator to run on propane.

3. Turn off unnecessary 12 volt appliances.

4. Record the time.

5. Shut off converter/charger (or unplug your RV if there is no way to switch off the converter/charger).

6. Run your 12 volt appliances and lights as you normally do.

7. Occasionally check the battery voltage with a digital volt meter and when you reach 12.25 volts which is approximately 50% of charge, turn your battery charger back on.

8. Check the time.

You now know how long you can run the RV, in "normal" use, without charging, before a "deep cycle" condition occurs.

Absorbed Glass Mat Battery – Pros & Cons

An Absorbed Glass Mat (AGM) battery is a type of battery that can be used as a starter battery or a deep cycle, but is not as good at either of these uses as ones designed for a specific purpose. It is a middle choice that gives you some of the benefits of both sides types of batteries.

A starter battery delivers a sudden, quick burst of energy such as is needed to start a motor. These batteries have a high CCA (Cold Cranking Amps) rating. They lose their charge level fast and should be recharged as soon as possible. Typically these live a life of being at or near 100% charge, losing down to the 70% level (while cranking the engine) and then being quickly charged back up by the engine's alternator. Starter batteries accept a charge fast. These batteries will run something such as a trolling motor, but not for as long as a deep cycle battery. You can use them as House Batteries in an RV, but they will discharge fast and wear out fast.

A deep cycle battery is made for long slow discharges, such as when running a golf car or as house batteries in an RV. They are often called Marine Batteries. They live a life of going from 100% charge slowly down to about 10%, then being slowly charged back up. It can take 24 hours to fully charge a deep cycle battery. In an emergency it can be used to crank the motor, but this will drain it fast.

The AGM battery falls in the middle. It works okay as a starting battery, but recharges slower than a high CCA starter battery. It can work as a house battery, but only works well down to about the 50% level, however an AGM battery charges faster than a true deep cycle battery. AGM batteries are sealed, no maintenance battery. It is about twice the cost of other batteries, but will also last longer.

All the electrolyte (acid) is contained in the glass mats. They cannot spill even if broken. There is no liquid to freeze and expand which makes them nearly immune to freezing damage.

Nearly all AGM batteries are "recombinant" which means the Oxygen and Hydrogen recombine inside the battery. The recombining is typically 99+% efficient, so almost no water is lost.

The charging voltages are the same as for any standard battery – no need for any special charging systems.

The internal resistance is extremely low so there is almost no heating of the battery even under heavy charge and discharge currents. Most AGM batteries have no charge or discharge current limits.

RV Quick Tips

RVer Tom 'Griz' Hiday provides today's quick tips.

✱ A motorhome has a number of vents and holes in the front that may let cold air in. I went to WallMart and bought some cheap black towels, (yes, they sell black ones!) and stuff them in places where I can feel cold air. This cuts down on heat loss in this area. The black towels are hard to see and I know what they are for.

✱ Most slides do not exactly seal perfectly. I stuff rags in these places too. These spots are not hard to find, I just wet my fingers and move them around. The cold spots are quickly evident.

RV Holding Tanks & Toilet Tips

RV Black Water Holding Tank Basics

Leave the black water tank valve closed and wait to dump the tank until it is at least two thirds full. You want the tank nearly full so that weight and gravity will force the contents out of the tank.

If the tank is not two thirds full when you're ready to dump then add water to the tank.

When the tank is empty, close the valve, add water to the tank… enough to cover the bottom, and treat with holding tank chemicals to assist in controlling odors.

RV Holding Tank Usage

If your RV is parked, and you have a sewer hook up, it's okay to leave the gray tank valve open, but you should leave the black tank closed. When the black tank is nearing the time when it needs to be emptied… the night before, close the valve on the gray tank and let it fill from use of the sinks and shower. The next day, open the black tank first and let it drain.

Most newer RV's have a built in black tank rinser. If your RV has one, connect a hose (NOT your drinking water white hose!) to the rinser and let it spray water in the black tank helping you flush it. The tank rinser hose connection should be near where the other water connections are.

If you do not have a built-in rinser you can get a toilet wand at your favorite RV store. Connect the wand to a hose and insert it down through the toilet into the black holding tank.

Once you have drained and rinsed the black tank, close that valve and add a couple of gallons of water and your favorite chemical.

Now open the gray tank valve. Be sure the black tank is closed before opening the gray tank valve. You do not want to mix contents between the two tanks.

As the gray tank empties, it will flush out the sewer hose of any residue from the black tank. Then leave the gray tank valve open again for daily use as it can fill fast when several people are using sinks and showering. If it fills, it will overflow into the lowest drain, which is usually the shower. This is not very pretty and can be quite stinky!

RV Holding Tank & Sewer Hose Tips

- If you use your RV more than a couple of weeks a year, spend a little extra money for heavy duty sewer hoses.

- Carry a garden hose along with your fresh water hoses. You can use it around the campsite, washing the rig, rinsing sewer hose, and the dump station if it doesn't have a hose available. Store the hose in an area away from your fresh water hose.

- When camping leave campground rest rooms and showers, the dump station, and the campsite as clean as you found them. Dispose of all trash properly.

- When hooking up at a new campsite, connect your RV water hose to the campground faucet first. Turn on the water and let it run for a while before hooking it up to your RV. This flushes the your water hose clean as well as water that has been standing inside the campground waterline. With water already in the hose you also eliminate most of the sputtering from your faucets.

- Never put anything other than black and gray water into a sewer drain.

- Never leave the black-water tank valve open when hooked up at a campground. Liquids will drain, solids will build up and harden on the bottom of the tank.

- Your black tank should be at least two thirds full before you dump. If you need to dump sooner simply add water to the tank first.

- When emptying your holding tanks, drain the black water tank first and then the gray water tank. This will help to clean the sewer hose out before you store it. It will also insure a good flow into the campgrounds sewer system.

- Local and state/province laws may require specific sewer connections. A sewer doughnut or threaded connector will cover most requirements so it's a good idea to have them onboard.

- The faucet at the dump station is for cleaning down the dump station area and your waste tanks after use. NEVER use it to fill your fresh water tanks.

- Carry at least two sewer hoses a 10 foot and a 20 foot length along with a hose coupling to join the lengths if needed, so you can reach 10 feet, 20 feet or 30 feet from your rig to the sewer as needed.

RV Macerator Pumps – the Basics

Macerator pumps provide a alternative to typical 'slinky hose' sewage disposal.

Macerator pumps chop black tank waste into a thin slurry so it can be pumped out through a 3/4 inch garden hose for proper disposal.

Many RVers use macerators in a temporary fashion when a normal sewer hookup is unavailable. This allows the them to pump sewage longer distances and into otherwise unavailable receptacles, like septic tanks, plumbing clean outs, sewers, or toilets.

Temporary hookups are done by attaching a macerator pump like the one made by Flojet to an RV sewage outlet just as you would a "slinky" sewer hose.

Some RVers have found that installing a macerator in a semi-permanent fashion is a better solution. Semi-permanence means the pump can be used without attaching and disconnecting but can be bypassed with valves for normal sewer hose connections. Carefully installed, a macerator can be used full-time with only a flick of the wrist and nary a drop of spillage.

A less expensive alternative to a macerator pump, called a jet pump, such as the Sewer Solution. It uses a jet of water supplied by a garden hose to create the slurry and 'pump' it through the supplied 3/4 inch hose.

Our Recent Experience With an RV Toilet

A member on our RV Basics discussion group wrote:

Our Thetford toilet, the one with the front flush pedal, overflowed inside the motorhome. This was clean water. The bowl just filled up and overflowed. Has anyone had this problem before and if so what do you do?

I think the fresh water connection on the back of the toilet is leaking but I can't see back there even with mirrors and flashlight much less get a wrench on it to tighten. Does anyone know how the toilet comes out where I can work on the problem...please.

Fran had the same experience with an RV toilet:

We have a Thetford toilet installed in the second bathroom of our Coachmen bunkhouse. We also had a leak… actually two, sometimes. Steve decided it must be the inflow valve and ordered a new one. This was probably a year ago. Yesterday we fixed it.

It wasn't a really big problem because the first leak was the inflow valve that leaked water into the toilet bowl. Trouble was, if I didn't watch it, it would fill up the bowl and overflow. We are full timers and most of the time are around the house to check on it. But I discovered that if I closed the flush valve slowly …with the foot pedal … the 'second' leak would let the water from the first leak leak into the holding tank. So we didn't really have to repair the inflow leak on an emergency basis. We waited until we got to Lancaster, the home of my #1 son Mark, who is very slim. If you would see the very small second bathroom in our bunkhouse model you would realize why his slimness was very important.

I read the instructions that came with the new valve, and I had also tried to see the workings on the back of the toilet with a mirror, but upside down and reversed was not helpful. The instructions sent with the replacement valve kit and flange from Thetford were helpful. They listed what we needed to gather up before we began the project: towels, plastic trash bag, one cross point screwdriver and another straight one, needle nose pliers and a half inch open end wrench.

Next was a list of what to do before beginning. This of course included the suggestion of draining the holding tank and using their Thetford holding tank deodorant but we skipped over that suggestion as well as the one where they wanted us to dress like an on-duty hazmat cleaning crew. I had already cleaned the toilet.

Now we were ready. Mark sent me to shut off the water where we were connected to his house.

There are usually two nuts bolting the toilet to the closet flange in the floor. Using the wrench Mark undid the bolts on either side. Not hard to find because the little white cover caps were not there. Turning the toilet around a bit he removed a black rubber O ring that holds the shroud together. The instructions said there were two but we only found one.

He removed three mounting screws, and a spring using the needle nose pliers then disconnected the water source from the old valve. This is where the towels came in handy. Just follow the step by step instructions. The process seemed so basic I probably could have done it myself except I couldn't fit in the space where Mark was working.

Reverse the process to install the new valve. Hook up the spring, replace the O ring, install the new seal flange on the base of the toilet and line up the holes with the bolts. Crank 'em down tight... but not too tight.

It's as easy as reading and following the directions ... and they offer those in three languages.

While we had the toilet unbolted we put a 2.5 inch riser under it ... but that's another tip.

RV Toilet Paper and Holding Tank Chemicals

There was an old man who used to get up at the crack of dawn every day and sprinkle white powder all around his yard. One day his neighbor's curiosity got the better of him so he asked the old man what he was sprinkling, he replied that it was elephant repellant. The neighbor nearly laughed himself unconscious. When he finally caught his breath he exclaimed "There are no elephants around here!" to which the old man answered "Yes I know, see how well the repellent works!"

It may not be the perfect analogy but I always think of that joke whenever the conversation turns to which is the best toilet paper or RV holding tank chemical.

Over the years I've heard of RVers using all kinds of stuff in their holding tanks — Pinesol, borax, liquid laundry detergent, Rid-ex, and even just two aspirin! I never could figure out how anyone would believe that two aspirin would deodorize and clean a 40+ gallon black tank. Each RVer would claim whatever concoction, including commercial RV chemicals, they use works better than all the rest. How is it possible? I believe that, just like the old man in the joke, RVers have a perception of a problem that doesn't really exist.

Now I will confess that I do use a tank chemical but only for odor control during the hot summer months... I found one that actually seems to work. But I don't worry about microbes or chemicals breaking down TP and solids. I simply don't believe 8 ounces of any chemical, home-brew or commercial, is going to have any significant effect in 45 gallons of waste. At least not in the few days it takes to fill my black tank.

I did have one of those clear plastic elbows for a while. It was good for seeing when the tank was empty or when you were flushing with fresh water to know when the tank was clean. But I never was able to distinguish any solids or lumps of TP in the flow that whooshed by when I pulled the valve. When the elbow finally broke I didn't replace it. With a 3 inch hose and the black tank flushing system I don't have to worry about all the 'stuff' in the tank. I works for me. But then, maybe the joke's on me.

As far as I know no one has ever seriously studied the effluent from a black tank close enough to really know if the chemical they use actually breaks down TP and solids. I know I'd rather not take on the job.

RV Quick Tip

✱ Not too many RVers use CB anymore but those who do say the radio has come in handy many times, especially around accident sites. To monitor traffic congestion on the road they listening to the truckers. Channel 19 has long been the "trucker channel" but truckers in specific areas may use a different channel.

RV Fresh Water System

There Are Two Ways to Get Fresh Water into the RV.

The first is a direct connection to a potable water supply. An example is when you are at a campsite with hookups. You simply attach your water hose to the spigot at your campsite, and connect the other end to the City Water inlet on your RV. Turn on the spigot and you have water to the faucets in your RV.

The other way is your freshwater tank. Usually the freshwater tank is filled through a gravity fill inlet. If you know that there won' t be a water supply at your campsite, then you'll want to fill your freshwater tank before you set out. When you need water, you'll need to turn on your water pump which draws water from the fresh water tank.

It's always a good practice to turn the water pump off if you're going to be away from your RV.

If you have a new or new-to-you RV, don't forget to sanitize your water system before you use it.

How to Sanitize the RV Fresh Water System

The generally accepted method of sanitizing your RV's fresh water system as outlined below involves filling the fresh water tank with a solution of household bleach and running the solution through each faucet. Then letting it stand for at least three hours. Finally, flush the system once or twice to remove the taste and smell.

- This procedure is one you'll find in most any book about RVing is tried and true but be sure to read on to find out what I do.

- Start with a nearly full fresh water tank.

- Turn the water heater off and let the water cool.

- Dilute one fourth cup of household bleach for each 15 gallons of tank capacity in a gallon of water.

- Add this chlorine/water solution to the fresh water tank.

- Add more water to the tank. The idea is to to mix the bleach solution throughout the tank.

- Open one faucet at a time. Let the chlorinated water run through each for one or two minutes. You should be able to smell the chlorine. (Make sure you are using the water pump and not the external water supply.)

- Top off the RV fresh water tank and let stand for at least three hours. Over night is better.

- Completely drain the system by opening the fresh water tank drain valve. Flushing the faucets for several minutes each will speed up emptying the tank. Open the hot water tank drain plug also and drain until it is empty.

- Close all valves, faucets and drain plugs.

- Fill water tank with fresh water.

- Flush each faucet for several minutes repeating until the tank is again empty. (Make sure you are using the water pump and not the external water supply.)

- The water should now be safe to drink but if the chlorine odor is too strong you can repeat the fresh water flush.

Traveling With a Full Fresh Water Tank

At about 8 pounds per gallon a full 45 gallon fresh water tank will weigh in at around 360 pounds. Whether the additional weight of a full fresh water tank makes a difference to you depends on the carrying capacity of your rig, how close you are to the maximum, how big your engine is and how you feel about always being prepared.

Few people will argue the more weight you carry the worse fuel mileage will be. However some RVers say they can't see any difference in fuel mileage with a full or empty tank.

The way we travel, it doesn't make much sense to have a full fresh water tank. Our travel days are usually less that 6 hours and we normally spend the night in an RV park with hookups. I try to keep a few gallons in the tank so we can use the restroom or wash up when we stop for lunch.

Even when a campground doesn't have water at the campsite there is usually water available and it's easy enough the fill the tank when arriving at the campground before setting up.

If I know we will be spending the night somewhere that doesn't have water I will fill the fresh water tank, or at least add more than usual, before we head out.

Of course, if we were going to travel the Loneliest Road in America or out across a desert I would probably fill the water tank.

RV Quick Tips

✱   Put wire screen in your rubber bumper plugs to prevent bees and wasps from nesting.

✱   When you finish up at the dump station, take a minute to make sure you haven't forgotten anything… gloves, pliers, sewer fittings and hose, and water hose. Be sure to lock your outside hatches before you leave.

RV Water Pump

When not connected to an external fresh water supply, fresh water can be obtained from the onboard water tank using an RV water pump. When power is switched on the pump functions automatically whenever a faucet is opened. It's normal for the pump to pulsate. Especially at low flow rates.

The water pump is preset to keep a more-or-less constant water pressure. When the pump senses a drop in pressure, because you're using water, it runs long enough to restore the pressure and then shuts off. Depending on the demand for water that pressure can be restored rapidly causing the pulsing.

You can install a device called an accumulator tank that will minimize the pulsating. There are RV water pump models available that claim to eliminate the pulsation and noise… ask your RV tech.

An Easy Fix for RV Water Heater Drip

Have you experienced water weeping or dripping from your water heater? Most likely the drip is coming from the pressure and temperature (P&T) relief valve as the water heater is operating. When the pressure of the water system gets too high the P&T valve will relieve the excess pressure.

The tank is designed to have an air pocket at the top that compresses as the water expands to keep the pressure within limits. Over time that air gets absorbed by the water and the water fills the tank.

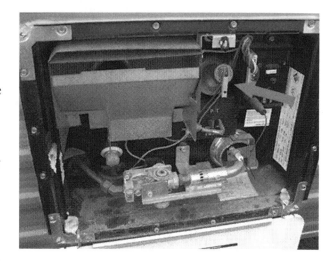

To replenish the air pocket:

- Turn off the water heater and let the water in the tank cool.

- Turn off the cold water supply line at the heater, if it is equipped with a valve, or turn off the water to the RV.

- Open a hot water faucet in the RV.

- Pull out the handle of the pressure P&T valve (see arrow) and allow water to flow from the valve until it stops.

- Release the handle on the P&T valve – it should snap closed.

The air pocket should be reestablished. Repeat this procedure when needed to minimize the weeping of the P&T valve.

RV Water Heater On or Off?

One question frequently asked by new RVers is should the RV water heater be left on always or only turned on when you need hot water.

There is no right or wrong answer so I'll offer some information that hopefully will make it easy for you to decide what will work best for you.

As full time RVers, Fran and I consider our RV our home and we treat it as such. Just as folks with a conventional house leave their water heater to operate unattended, so do we.

For us, it's a real pain to discover, just when you're ready to take a shower, that we forgot to switch on the water heater. It happens more often than not when we have tried to conserve electricity and propane by 'temporary' use of the water heater.

Our water heater can operate either on propane, electric or both. We usually just let the electric element heat the water since it does a good job and doesn't use up our propane. During the summer though, when we're running the air conditioner along with all the computers, TVs, microwave oven, ice maker etc., the addition of the water heater electric element is enough to trip the 30 amp circuit breaker. So, sometimes it's necessary for us to switch off the electric heater and switch on the propane. It's easy enough, the two switches are handy.

When we need to heat water quickly we will switch on both the electric and propane.

Some RVers will switch on the RV water heater only before they need it. If you're organized enough to know ahead of time you'll need hot water that's perfectly okay. The water heater tank is fairly well insulated and the water can stay warm for several hours depending on how cold it is outside. Warm water is all you really need to wash your hands or an occasional dish or two. When you need to wash many dishes or take a shower you'll have to wait until the water has heated.

One RVer wrote that a person in their family used oxygen so they were concerned about the propane flame on the heater. They never used the heater unless the person was out of the RV. This is an unfounded fear.

The flame of the water heater, and the furnace for that matter, is vented to the outside of the RV and well isolated from the interior. This is why you can use the heater without fear of carbon monoxide poisoning.

Some RVers complain the water heater is too noisy. This can be a legitimate complaint if the water heater is on the curb side and you are sitting outside next to it. If the burner sounds like a blast furnace you should have the burner adjusted. A properly adjusted burner shouldn't be that noisy.

Lastly, some RVers simply believe they are conserving propane and electricity by only heating water when needed. Others argue the energy used to get the water up to temperature each time you turn on the heater is greater than what is used to just keep it hot. I believe the latter but, to my knowledge, there has not been a scientific study to prove which camp is right so you'll just have to decide that question for yourself. Extreme outside temperature may adjust your thinking one way or the other.

Water Pump Check Valve Repair & Tips

The fresh water tank in our previous fifth wheel started filling on it's own. I noticed water dripping under the trailer and determined it was coming from an over-full fresh water tank. I knew the last time I looked it was near empty and I didn't fill it. I drained the tank and watched as it refilled over a period of a few days.

The problem was a bad check valve on the water pump. The valve is meant to prevent city water from leaking into the fresh water tank. When this little-known part fails it allows water to flow backward through the pump into the freshwater tank anytime you're hooked up to city water.

The fix is easy and you can probably do it yourself. Parts are available at any well-stocked RV parts store. Repair the check valve... or replace the complete pump if it's old and you use it a lot.

In my case the fix above wasn't an option. The water pump was in a place with difficult access. For a water pump we seldom used and which still actually worked, I didn't want to spend the time and effort needed to get at it. Instead of repairing the pump I put another check valve in the water line at a place I could reach. The pump and the check valve were still working when we sold the rig.

While I'm talking about check valves, the water heater in our new fifth wheel had a check valve go bad. Every time we used the hot water we would hear a buzz. But that's another tip of the day.

Tips to minimize RV water pump noise.

To minimize RV water pump noise/vibration you should have at least one foot of **flexible high pressure tubing** connecting both the inlet and outlet ports of the pump. This helps keep the pump's normal oscillations from being transmitted to the rigid plastic pipes in the RV.

A more expensive way to reduce water pump noise is to replace your old pump with a variable speed pump. While these pumps cost $50 to $75 more than typical water pumps installed in RVs they dramatically reduce hammer and vibration.

You can also consider installing an accumulator tank. It's a pressure storage vessel with a bladder inside... air on one side of the bladder and water on the other. Because air can be compressed the accumulator absorbs some of the pump pressure when it pulses making water flow more steady and the pump work more efficiently. The accumulator tank also provides additional water storage to assist the pump in meeting the total demands of the plumbing system.

De-Winterizing The RV Fresh Water System

De-winterizing your RV's fresh water system involves removing all traces of the RV antifreeze used to protect the water system.

- Put several gallons of water into the fresh water tank.

- Turn on the on-board water pump, and open a cold water tap. Allow the water to flow for several minutes.

- Connect the water hose to your city water supply inlet. Turn on the supply.

- Open all cold water taps one by one and allow the water to flow water until it is clear of anti-freeze..

- Flush the toilet until the water is clear of anti-freeze.

- Open the water heater bypass and fill the water heater with fresh water. Allow a few gallons to flow through the water heater by running water through all the hot water faucets one faucet at a time.

RV Quick Tips

✱ Call to check for RV size restrictions at campgrounds before you get there. Particularly sites at state and national parks and also older private campgrounds.

✱ Many vhehicle used in cold climates have engine preheaters built in. You can usually find a male end of an extension cord in the engine comparment if a heater is installed. To prevent this plug becoming corrode or coated with dirt and oil, put a female plug on that to keep it clean.

RV Electrical System Tips

RV Shore Power Safety

Most RVers take RV Shore Power safety for granted. After all, the power pedestals were installed and wired by licensed electricians right? It's the law... there are building codes right?

I once sat and watched as the park 'maintenance' man reversed the polarity on the outlet at the next site because the RVer complained he had low voltage.

At another park I got a nice tingle whenever I reach for the door handle of the RV.

You can guard against plugging your RV into an improperly wired power pedestal with a simple, inexpensive polarity checker.

Most common polarity checkers have a standard household 15-amp plug. To test 30-amp or 50-amp outlets you need the appropriate adaptor.

Of course, proper voltage is as important as proper polarity, and you can check that with another inexpensive item.

Check the power outlet for voltage and polarity at your new site before you settle in. That way it won't be too much trouble to move to another site if there is a problem.

It's not necessary but if you have a spare outlet in your RV, preferable one you can check easy, leave the voltage meter plugged in to monitor to voltage. During the summer, when everyone is running their air conditioner, the voltage at many parks can drop below the acceptable level.

Ground Fault Interrupt Outlet

If some or all of the 120 volt AC outlets in your RV are dead and you have checked the circuit breakers and they seem to be fine it's time to check the GFI outlet to see if it has been tripped.

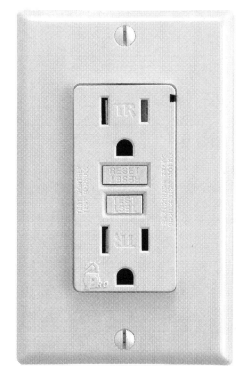

GFI stands for Ground Fault Interrupt. It may also be called a Ground Fault Circuit Interrupt (GFCI) outlet.

A GFI outlet is designed to provide protection from electrocution. In most RVs you will find a GFI outlet on the circuit that provides power to the kitchen, bathroom and outside outlets. Only one GFI outlet is needed to protect an entire circuit. Your RV may have all the outlets on one circuit or there may be two or more circuits. If you have multiple circuits you may have more that one GFI outlet... one on each circuit.

GFI outlets work by measuring the flow of electricity in both the hot (black) and neutral (white) wire. If the two are not equal, then there is a ground fault and the breaker inside the outlet disconnects the power.

There are two buttons on a GFI outlet. They may be colored but not always. One button is a TEST button. As you may have guessed, pressing the test button checks the outlet for proper function. If the outlet is working properly the GFI will trip and all outlets on the circuit will be dead.

The other button on the GFI outlet is the RESET and pressing it will, of course, reset the GFI and restore power to all outlets on the circuit.

Keep in mind that while the GFI outlet reduces the chance of electrocution it does not guarantee it. All precautions should still be taken.

RV 30 amp Power Management

Our first fifth wheel, as well as our current one, is wired for 30 amp service. For the most part that's adequate for our needs. When we started out it didn't take us long to learn that 30 amp service has it's limitations. Especially in the summer when we need the air conditioner.

There are several appliances on most RVs that few newbies consider, the 1500 watt roof air conditioner which draws around 12 amps, the heating element in the refrigerator draws about the same when it's on electric as does the electric heating element in the water heater.

Most larger RVs are wired with two circuits, usually one circuit down each side, with a 20 amp breaker protecting each circuit. Any two of the appliances above running on a circuit will likely trip a 20 amp breaker. For example, if you have the air conditioner on and decide to use the microwave on that circuit, you will likely trip the breaker.

Keep in mind that though you are able to run up to 20 amps on a circuit you will have to limit usage to 10 amps on the other circuit since the RV itself is protected by a 30 amp circuit breaker. Fortunately, RV manufacturers generally balance amperage requirements between circuits. For example, they may place the air conditioner on a circuit with a string of outlets while the other circuit will have the refrigerator, water heater and kitchen outlets.

To get a better handle on what your appliance load is, check the owners manuals you have or the stickers on the appliances to see the watts or amps they have listed. Watts divided by volts gives amps used. Shore power is 120 volts (or thereabouts) so a 700 Watt microwave is drawing about 6 amps. It takes a little math, but it is simple math.

You may trip a breaker a few times until you learn what combination of appliances you can run at the same time but it's not rocket science and you'll soon learn how to live within the limitations. Try humming the 'Green Acres' theme song.

Converter? Inverter? Confused?

A converter is standard equipment on most RVs… certainly modern RVs. Connected to a campground power pedestal or when your RV generator is running the converter changes 120 Volt AC power to 12 Volt DC and supplies power to the RV's 12v circuits and charges the RV batteries.

Inverters take 12VDC from the batteries and change it to 120VAC. Depending on the wattage rating of the inverter most 120 Volt AC electric items may be operated without plugging into shore power or running a generator. Although many RVs now come equipped with inverters they are not generally standard equipment so, if you want one, be sure you specify that if you are ordering an RV from the factory. Of course you can always have one installed.

RV Power Inverter Do's & Don'ts

DO yourself a favor and gather information. Flea markets are littered with useless, cheap inverters that people thought were bargains.

DO read the instructions carefully, more than once, and highlight the critical steps before attempting to connect an inverter. Some have elaborate instructions (good), but critical safety precautions are buried in the text and easily overlooked.

DO locate the power inverter as close to the batteries as possible. Use as heavy a cable as possible (read the instructions).

DO ventilate the power inverter well. They can get very warm. They need fresh air, just like a stereo or computer. Inverters do well in outside RV compartments as long as they are protected from the elements.

DO consider a small power inverter if it suits the need. Unless your wiring is inadequate, you can plug small inverters... 100 - 200 watts... into standard 12VDC receptacles. This avoids installation issues and saves money.

DO consider load transfer switches for larger power inverters even though they may cost more. If you also have a generator, make sure the transfer switch will handle three sources of power. shore power, generator power and inverter power.

DO make sure you know what you're doing when wiring an RV power inverter, or get help from someone who does. Even if you use a professional electrician, make sure he understands that neutral and ground wires in an RV are NOT bonded together.

DO consider a power inverter a for your RV a priority item if medical appliances keep you tied to commercial power. (You can even plug the small ones into wheel chair batteries in many cases.)

DO buy a power inverter from a dealer who can advise you before you purchase.

DO buy a power inverter from a company that will let you return it for full (or nearly full) credit if it's in like new condition, original box, etc. Some inverters will cause radio/TV interference. Some will cause interference only on certain brands or models within brands. Good dealers will allow you to take your RV to their place of business so inverters can be temporarily connected to test interference problems.

DON'T be afraid of RV power inverters. They're perfectly safe if used properly. They're not difficult to install if you follow the instructions. They can just about pay for themselves depending on what you use them for.

DON'T ever attempt to connect the power inverter to your electrical system with a simple jumper cord using a male connector (plug) at each end. The chance of shock or shorting the power invert is too great. And you will damage the inverter.

Reader Comment:

After I got rained on while checking the batteries under the interior steps, I swapped the contents. Now the batteries are on a slide out in the old inverter compartment and the inverter is under the steps. I cut additional vents into the fiberglass compartment and covered them with HVAC screens. They are placed on the side and back of the compartment to aid in air flow. Didn't have to extend any cables but did add additional cable clamps (insulated aircraft wiring clamps) to ensure things stayed in place. I like the idea of the batteries being on a slide out and easily checked and maintained. Thought this would be an idea for others.

Solar Power is Ideal for RVs

Use the sun to charge your RV batteries. RVs use mostly 12 volt direct current electricity. This makes them a perfect application for solar panels.

RV solar panel systems consist of as many as five panels installed on the roof of the RV where the sun can shine on them. The system connects to your batteries through a controller and charges them during the day.

The advantage to RV solar systems is silence and there are no moving parts, just the sun shining on the panels. You'll never know they are even there.

The disadvantage is the relatively high initial cost… about $2500 to $4000 for a multi-panel system. You'll probably want a larger battery bank as well as an inverter to run 120 volt appliances.

Compared to the cost of a generator and it's ongoing cost, you may well decide a solar system is a better choice.

Tip for Installing and Using Solar Panels

Plan on a solar charging system that will replace what you use from your batteries PLUS 10%. That's because anytime energy is transformed there is some loss.

- Your solar panel system should include metering and regulating devices.

- An average RV couple can meet most of their needs with three, full-size modules and two batteries. However, this rule of thumb can vary widely depending on your lifestyle.

- Just because you have a 105AH "rated" battery, don't think you can get 105AH out of it. Ideally, you shouldn't use more than 20% (resting voltage of 12.5) of a battery's rated capacity if you want it to last. That's about 20+ amp hours a day. You can take 50% (resting volts of 12.3) out of a battery safely. But you must recharge it fully as soon as possible. Using more than 50% is a "deep cycle," and a battery is only good for so many of them.

- You can increase solar panel output by tilting them toward the sun. If you mount them on the RV so they tilt, but can't be rotated, then you'll have to rotate the RV. Sometimes you can't do that. The simpler way to get more power is to add an extra panel (or two) and leave them lying flat.

- Spend time figuring out where to put panels and building quality mounts for them. You'll save in the long run with no leaks, no damage and maximum output.

- Don't skimp on wire size, proper connectors or the equipment itself. You'll ultimately be sorry if you do.

- You can install a solar system successfully with no more information than is in the basic instructions, or you can pay someone to do it for you. But, you won't have the faintest idea what's going on. On the other hand, you can read a few, simple books, make a hobby out of the whole thing and learn many neat tricks. How many hobbies pay for themselves?

- Some RV manufacturers are now "roughing in" solar panel wiring or even offering whole system installation. But, many are skimpily wired, thus defeating the whole idea. You must know what questions to ask.

Travel Trailer Plug Preventive Maintenance

Always check your travel trailer lights before you hit the road. If they don't work, one possible cause is dirt or oxidation on the umbilical cord plug and/or receptacle contact points.

Make it a habit to clean the contacts with a wire brush or sandpaper. A Dremel tool with a small wire brush will make the job easier (be sure the lights are off when you do this, otherwise it could blow a fuse).

Scrape off dirt and corrosion in the contact holes with an ice pick, rat-tail file or small piece of sandpaper rolled around a toothpick Then, dab a little grease on the prongs, push the connector together.

A little petroleum jelly or light waterproof grease spread on the surfaces will act as a barrier against air and moisture, retard oxidation and keep the lights operating longer.

Soldering all wire splices will help prevent problems with loose connections. Wrapping the splices tightly with electrical tape or heat-shrink tubing will seal out dirt and eliminate shorts.

To keep dirt from getting into the plug between uses slip a small plastic bag over the plug and secure it with a rubber band or tape.

Emergency Flasher for RV Travel Trailer Marker Lights

Your travel trailer or fifth wheel is broken down on the side of the road at night and you want to take your truck into town for parts or to get help. Wouldn't it be nice if you could leave the trailer marker lights on? Since flashing lights mean caution or emergency it would be even better if you could make them flash.

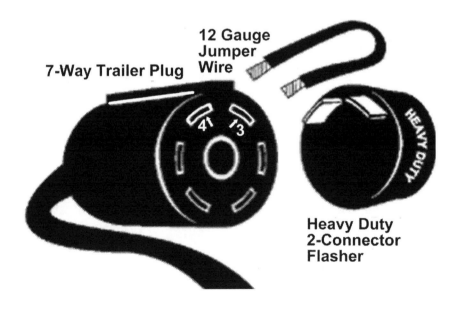

12 Gauge Jumper Wire

7-Way Trailer Plug

Heavy Duty 2-Connector Flasher

I've seen instructions for an emergency flasher that requires you to purchase a female connector, do some soldering and wrap the lash up with electrical tape. Well, as you will see from the illustration below, this way is so easy that anyone can do it and all it takes is a heavy duty 2-pin flasher available at any auto parts store.

Depending on how many lights your rig has you may need more than a typical Heavy Duty flasher you can buy at the auto parts store. I hat to get mine at a truck stop.

The key is to connect the flasher to your trailer's umbilical plug as shown in the illustration. See how the plug is oriented with the square bump at the top. Notice the two white arrows pointing to the top two pins of the plug. The pin on the left is #4 and is the battery charging line. The right pin, #3, supplies power to the license, tail and running lights.

When you want the lights on but not flashing… we use our running lights as makeshift Christmas and party lights… just use a short length of 12 gauge wire as a jumper to light up your rig.

RV Quick Tips

✱   If the refrigerator has an unpleasant odor consider a commercial odor remover. Spray into the refrigerator and close the door. Repeat if necessary. Wash the interior before loading with food.

✱   A common "warning" for the RV TV antenna is a clothes pin. When you put the antenna up, remove the clothes pin from the crank and clip it on the gearshift. When you crank the antenna down, move the pin back to the crank. You could use different colored pins for different reminders.

RV Refrigerator Tips

How Level is Level Enough for an RV Refrigerator

One of the several frequently asked questions often discussed on the RVbasics Yahoo Group is how level does an RV refrigerator have to be for proper operation and to avoid damaging the cooling unit.

It used to be that an RV refrigerator had to be near perfect level to avoid serious damage to the cooling unit. But modern-day RV refrigerators are no longer as susceptible to damage due to operation at less than perfect level. Unfortunately, the 'old truth' continues to be passed from the veteran RVers to the newbies.

To set the record straight, the text below was taken from a Dometic RV refrigerator owners manual.

In recent years Dometic has engineered a new type of cooling unit that utilizes an improved siphon pump tube design which drastically reduces the possibility of permanent damage to the coils if operated in an out-of-level condition, or too much heat is generated at the boiler section. The siphon pump tube is enclosed in the design and is surrounded by a weak ammonia solution, which will protect the pump tube from abnormally over-heating. This type of unit; however, does not eliminate the need for proper leveling. The unit still requires gravitational flow to provide the proper cooling process, and if leveling is outside the necessary limits, cooling will dramatically slow down or stop completely.

- *The cooling coils are not normally damaged in this fashion and once proper leveling is maintained, the cooling process will resume.*

- *Spirit or bubble levels are no longer being supplied with the new style refrigerators as the RV or vehicle only needs to be leveled so it is comfortable to live in, with no noticeable sloping of the floor or walls. For diagnosis, the new style cooling units that incorporate the protection boiler system, can be differentiated from the older style coils by the shape and design of the outer boiler box cover on the rear of the cooling unit. These new units will incorporate a circular metal cover, while the older style refrigerator utilizes a square shaped boiler enclosure.*

The above also holds true for Norcold brand RV Refrigerators.

While the refrigerator should be level when the vehicle is stationary, performance during transit is not normally affected.

RV Refrigerator: Propane or Electric?

RV refrigerators don't work the same way a conventional home unit does. Your RV unit uses heat to create a chemical reaction which, through evaporation and then condensation, cools the cold box.

The primary heat source for RV refrigerators is a small propane burner. Most units also include a 120 volt AC electric heating element for use when the RV is hooked up to campground shore power.

When you are not hooked up to shore power you will need to operate on propane. In camp, with shore power, it's a matter of choice as to which you use; propane or 120 volt. You may prefer electricity simply because it increases the time between propane fill-ups. However a refrigerator uses very little propane compared to a water heater or furnace.

Traveling with the RV Refrigerator On or Off?

There is never ending debate among RVers about whether to travel with the refrigerator operating on propane.

After hearing both sides of the debate, I can tell you there is no real consensus and both sides are adamant in their beliefs. As far as I can tell there is no right or wrong answer, it's up to you to decide what's right for you.

If you decide to travel with the refrigerator on using propane be sure to turn if off before stopping for fuel.

If you travel less than four to five hours a day you should be able turn your refrigerator off and it will stay cold enough to keep your food fresh. You can even briefly open the door to get lunch or a cold drink if you don't open it too many times.

If you decide to travel with the refrigerator off here are some tips for keeping things cold.

- Start the refrigerator early the day before you plan to travel.

- Put already cold foods, soft drinks and beer etc. in the refrigerator the night before.

- Pack the refrigerator full. Use the cold drinks to fill space.

- Pack the freezer full.

- Make sure everything is cold before you turn the refrigerator off for travel.

- Plan ahead... know what you want before you open the door and get everything you want at one time.

Humidity Switch on Dometic RV Refrigerators

Many Dometic brand RV refrigerators are equipped with a humidity switch. The humidity switch powers a small heating element around the freezer door. The purpose is to control frost that may collect during very high humidity situations.

The heating element is not on the refrigerator on/off switch, So as long as the humidity switch is on the heating element is drawing power even if the refrigerator is turned off.

The heating element draws around 6 amps that will drain a battery in just a few hours. If your battery goes down for no apparent reason, check this switch!

Turn the RV Refrigerator into a Message Center

Space in your RV at a premium? Looking for a handy place to pin up your grocery and to-do lists? Want to display the latest photographs and artwork of the grandkids? Consider your refrigerator doors.

The decorative panels on the refrigerator doors are easy to remove and can be replaced with a cork board, a white board or sheet metal ...if you are into refrigerator magnets.

You can find all three of these type boards at your local office supply store.

You can make your own white board with a smooth, glossy finish (to write on with dry erase pens) from a piece of plain shower board found at home supply stores.

Be sure you measure your door panel before you go to the store so you get a board large enough. Chances are that what you buy will need to be cut to size. If you're not comfortable cutting the board yourself you can most likely find a cabinet maker who will cut a cork board or wallboard. You may need to find a sheet metal shop to cut steel panel to size.

To finish up you will need push pins for a cork board, dry erase pens for a white board and magnets for the sheet metal. Refrigerator magnets are fun, collectible souvenirs of your travels. Get a couple 4 x 4 or 4 x 6 inch notepads with the sticky border on the page backs. Remove ten or twelve sheets from the front of the pad and stick them on your new bulletin board for your next grocery list.

RV Quick Tips

* Use Checklists. It's easy to forget to do something! Roof vents, steps TV antennas, and storage compartments left unlocked are just some of the things most often forgotten.

* Check tire pressure before every trip. The most frequent cause of tire failure is under inflation.

* Emergency Roadside Assistance is worth every penny and can save you hundreds of dollars. Read why we like Good Sam ERS.

* Consider joining a Discount Camping Club. Depending on your RVing lifestyle it is possible to save up to 50% on campsite fees. Check them out carefully as they are not right for everyone.

* For permanent electrical connections consider using liquid electrical tape. It is a rubber insulation coating that has excellent acid, alkaline and abrasion protection and seals out moisture and salt permanently. The rubber based coating will not harden, unravel or become brittle in extreme weather conditions.

RV Roof Air Conditioner Tips

RV Roof Air Conditioner Gasket Leaks

An RV roof air conditioner sits on a large foam gasket and is held in place by four bolts or threaded rods and nuts that go through the A/C vent to the inside ceiling frame. This mounting method isolates much of the A/C vibration making it quieter running.

Over time the gasket will compress and the fastening bolts/nuts will become loose.

When this happens water leaks, either from rain or condensation from the operating air conditioner, can occur at the gasket. Fortunately the leak can usually be stopped by simply tightening the nuts/bolts. Don't tighten them too much, just snug them, you still want the gasket to have some give.

If you can't stop the leak by tightening the bolts, the gasket may be damaged or just too old, so you will want to replace it.

Replacing an A/C gasket can be strenuous… a roof A/C unit is pretty heavy… but it's an easy project. Simply remove the fastening nuts/bolts, disconnect the wiring harness, go up on the roof and lift/tilt the air conditioner off the vent… it's easier when two people do it. You should have someone down below to make sure wires and such don't get hung up.

New gaskets don't need added putty and stuff, but you do need to make sure the roof edges around the vent are clean and don't have gouges or dents through which water can leak.

RV Roof Air Conditioner Freezing Up

There is a sensor that is attached to the condenser of the RV air conditioner that will detect when the condenser is too cold and turn off the compressor to prevent the condenser freezing up.

When the air conditioner on our new fifth wheel was freezing up my RV tech suggested that I look to see of the sensor was properly installed… it was not.

After attaching it to the condenser the air conditioner works properly and does not freeze.

Also, when looking for the sensor, I noticed the intake and exhaust were not properly partitioned which allowed much of the cold air to be immediately recycled rather than going out through the ducting. Several strips of duct tape fixed that and the RV air conditioner is much more efficient now.

RV Air Conditioner Heating Element

Some roof top recreational vehicle air conditioners, for example Coleman brand RV air conditioners have a heating element or 'heat strip' installed which is intended to be used as a supplement to the RV furnace. If you don't have one installed it's likely an option. The heating element is the equivalent in capacity to a small portable electric heater… about 1500 watts.

It's generally used to take the chill off the air rather the heat the RV. You can use it when your furnace isn't working to get you through a cold night. You may not be toasty warm but you won't freeze either.

Heat Pumps and Air Conditioners: What's the Difference?

Simply stated, an air conditioner will cool your vehicle while a heat pump can operate in both a heating and cooling mode.

In air conditioners the refrigerant flows in one direction and is optimized to cool. With heat pumps, the refrigerant flows in either direction depending on whether to unit is heating or cooling. When the refrigerant is reversed the condenser becomes the evaporator and the evaporator works as the condenser. That the basic description, it's a little more complicated in actuality.

Troubleshooting RV Air Conditioners

Setting the thermostat on a low temperature setting and the fan on low speed in high humidity situations can cause evaporator freeze-up. Turn the air conditioner off to allow the the evaporator to defrost.

If the air conditioner/heat pump doesn't run (the fan and/or the compressor), check the AC voltage. Look at the breaker in the electrical panel.

Check for 12-volts at the thermostat. The 12-volt DC fuse should be checked.

When the fan runs and the compressor tries to start but won't run, check the RV's power cord, plug and receptacle. If those are in working order, check the AC voltage. Inside your RV. Uss a plug-voltmeter or connect the leads of a voltmeter to a receptacle and start your air conditioner or heat pump. Once the compressor has been running for two minutes, check your voltage. It must be at least 103.5 volts for the air conditioner to operate.

If the fan runs, but the compressor cycles on and off and doesn't cool correctly, it could be poor air flow due to a dirty filter, dirty condenser or a duct leak. Low AC voltage may also be the problem.

RV Propane Tips

RV Propane Cylinder Re-certification

If you have an older Travel Trailer or Fifth Wheel you should know that according to Federal law, DOT cylinders may only be used for 12 years after their manufacture date. After that, the cylinders must be "re-certified" which provides another five years of use. The cylinders can be re-certified every five years thereafter.

Check the date stamped on your cylinders... don't rely on your rig's model year even if the cylinders are original. It's quite possible they are a year or more older than your rig. Ours were.

Propane venders are legally required to look at the date stamped on the cylinder before filling it. Some actually do look. We've been reminded a few times that our cylinders were about to expire.

Re-certification is usually done by the large bulk propane suppliers but our local RV repair shop was certified to do the job and they did it for free as a customer service! Call around to see who may do it in your area.

LPG (Liquid Propane Gas) Leak Detector Operation and Safety Tips

All RVs should have a propane gas leak detector. It is typically located about 3 inches above the floor, usually near the side door or in the kitchen area. While you should regularly check your RV LPG system for proper operation, if a leak should occur and LPG enters the inside of the RV, the alarm will sound. LPG is heavier than air and will concentrate in a layer on the floor until it reaches the LPG detector.

If the alarm should sound, push the black switch down into the OFF position, open the windows and doors and exit the RV. Close the valve on the propane cylinder and allow the cabin to air out.

When you feel it safe to re-enter, try to find out what is wrong. If all seems okay, put the switch on the leak detector back into the ON position. The alarm may sound for 30-60 seconds but if the gas is gone the alarm will stop and a green light will begin blinking. Now you can use the LPG system again.

The LPG detector is powered by the coach/auxiliary battery. The detector will operate to detect gas and sound an alarm until the auxiliary battery is drained as low as 9 volts. (The LOW battery light indicates 10.4 volts.)

On some RVs, the LPG detector is both an alarm and an automatic main cutoff for LPG. When the alarm sounds, the LPG supply to the vehicle is shut off. When the coach battery has less than 9 volts charge, the gas will be turned off. The only way to reset the detector and restore the gas service is to bring your auxiliary battery back up to at least 11 volts.

Propane Cylinder Filling Methods

Propane cylinder filling methods vary by company and region.

Filling Propane Cylinders By Weight

Along with a visual inspection of the exterior, the cylinder filler will look for two weights stamped on the cylinder prior to setting the cylinder on the scale and connecting the fill hose. These two weights are the water capacity and tare weight. The water capacity (WC) is how much water the propane cylinder will hold in pounds. The tare weight or empty weight indicated by a "TW" is what the cylinder weighs when empty.

The cylinder filler will generally have a cylinder filling chart that converts water capacity to pounds of propane that he will refer to before filling the cylinder. The chart will show, for example, that 47.6 pounds of water converts to 20 pounds of propane. With a tare weight of 18 pounds the scale would to be set to 38 pounds (20 lbs + 18 lbs = 38 lbs) to match the weight of the cylinder when it is full.

After the scale is set and the fill nozzle is attached to the cylinder valve, the attendant may open the bleeder valve, reset the meter and begin pumping propane into the cylinder. The attendant will stop the pump when:

- The bleeder valve starts to spew liquid

- The scale indicates the cylinder has reached its capacity

- The OPD (Overfill Protection Device) valve stops the flow of propane into the cylinder

Some fillers may load your filled cylinder into your vehicle while some, for liability reasons, will not . So don't be offended if you have to load your own cylinder.

Filling Propane Cylinders By Meter

In many places propane cylinders are simply filled using a meter on the pump much like the fuel pump at a gas station. The fill is charge by the gallon as indicated on the meter.

The attendant will stop the pump once:

- The bleeder valve starts to spew liquid

- The meter indicates the cylinder has reached its capacity

- The OPD (Overfill Protection Device) valve stops the flow of propane into the cylinder

Filling and Charging a Flat Fee

Charging a flat fee may be charged on small cylinders when the company determines the cost of labor is more than any profit made from selling the propane. You should know in advance that you may be charged the full amount even if the cylinder isn't completely empty. I have never experienced this personally.

Post Winter Propane Check

If you stored your RV over the winter the propane gas system may develop some air in the lines. When taking your RV out storage it's a good idea to purge the air and check that everything is working properly. You should perform the following check well in advance of your planned vacation to allow time for any repairs.

- Open the propane cylinder valves.

- Light one of the stovetop burners. This purges the most of the air from the system and is a visual check that propane is present.

- Once the stove burner flame is steady, light all burners and check for a consistent blue flame. Turn off the stove burners and light the oven. It should burn with a blue flame. Turn off the oven.

- Check the water heater, furnace and refrigerator. Make sure the refrigerator and water heater are set to operate on propane as you check for proper operation.

RV Propane Detector Sounds False Alarm

If the propane detector in your RV sounds even though you're sure there is no leak it could be defective but most likely it is just a low battery.

Your RV's propane detector is powered by the coach battery. If the voltage in the battery is too low the detector will sound.

Fully charge the battery. If the detector sounds you may have a defective unit but have it checked by an RV shop before you replace it.

If the Detector sounds when the propane is on then you have to get an RV shop to check the entire system for leaks.

One other possibility, the detector can be set off by different sprays such a hairspray and deodorants. Often times these and other spays use propane as the propellant.

RV Quick Tips

✱ When you are hitched up and ready to pull out, take just a few minutes and double check everything.

✱ Walk around and out to the edge of your campsite to get a different view of the RV and to spot anything that didn't get packed away and any trash that needs to be picked up.

✱ Plan your day's travel so that you don't have to drive during rush hour traffic. Try to be off the road long before evening commute traffic starts.

✱ Clean off the top of your slide-outs before closing them up.

RV Modification Tips

Making Your RV House an RV Home

Just because your RV came with certain things in certain places doesn't mean that is the way it has to be. Making your house a home is part of the fun. If you are a part-time RVer you are probably more apt to put up with your rig the way you got it, but if you are a full time RVer you have probably found many things you'd like to have different.

We bought our second fifth wheel because we mostly liked the floor plan. We had lived full-time in our old fifth wheel long enough to have a good idea what we wanted.

The new fifth wheel was a bunkhouse model that was advertised to sleep 12. We don't even know 12 people well enough to sleep that closely with them, but it had lots of space.

Fran's area: The 'bunk' room over the fifth wheel end was set up with 4 bunks to sleep 6 young people. We removed three of the bunks and raised the fourth to a more adult-useable height. We fixed a shelf for my dulcimers and fiddle, a set of sturdy plastic drawers for some of my clothes, my computer work station, printer, TV, etc. The small bathroom would be a nice closet, but I would much rather have the second bathroom which came with the rig. We added a 2.5″ podium to the toilet to make the height a little more comfortable.

Steve's area: The rear of the rig has the other toilet, a shower, bed, a closet and some built in drawers and overhead cabinets, TV, etc. He found a wood counter top at a home center that made the built-in dresser into a small desk he uses for his computer. He also added a small shelf to hold some external computer disk drives.

In the great room: The cushion on one of the dinette benches was removed to make room for a counter-top ice maker and a bread machine.

We decorated the over head cabinets with wooden love spoons Steve carved and they look so at home that people think they surely came with the decor of the rig. Kitchen counter space and the entertainment center are still in the thought process. We haven't traded out the 'hide-a-bed' couch yet, but we did replace the padding in the back cushions of the couch to make it more comfy.

We've added to our great room art pieces from artist friends, a toy fifth wheel/truck and an atomic clock.

Wire racks make good use of extra tall overhead storage space, for table ware, small appliances, snacks, etc. as well as cans, jars and boxes in too-tall pantry shelves.

The point is that you can redecorate and modify your rig just as you may have done in your sans wheel house. Certainly if you decide to replace something like a couch, recliner chair or other large item, make sure the new one will fit through the door. Also if you do any interior painting be sure to choose a time and place where you can leave the doors and windows open for ventilation.

There are many cosmetic upgrades you can do that shouldn't affect your warranty. If you have doubts, call the manufacturer's customer service line and ask.

Add-Ons That Make RV Life Better

RVers usually make changes and add things to their RVs that make living and traveling in the RV better and more convenient. Bellow are a few of the modifications and add-on we've done to our fifth wheel.

- Small portable ice maker. We use it all year long. We could never make enough ice cubes in the freezer… especially in the summer months. We used to buy a bag of ice about every two days. Problem with that was there wasn't enough room in the freezer for frozen foods. Our portable ice maker solved both problems.

- A second bedroom and bathroom. They came with the rig... a bunkhouse model fifth wheel. We removed three of the four bunks and modified one.

- A curved shower curtain rod. We don't have a tub. The shower stall glass surround leaked so we need to use a shower curtain. Removed the glass surround and replaced it with a curved rod and some well placed velcro. A lot lighter than the glass surround.

- An electric powered holding tank dump valve on the forward black tank. We no longer have to crawl under the rig to dump.

- Lined the wheel wells of the fifth wheel with heavy gauge sheet metal so blowouts won't tear up the subfloor (again).

- The plastic panels in the screen door obscured the view when looking out while sitting in the living room. Replacing the opaque panels with clear plastic ones improved the view considerably.

RV Quick Tips

✱ When merging into traffic or changing lanes, match the speed of traffic as closely as possible. This makes it possible to enter the traffic lane into a smaller opening and is far safer than expecting the traffic to slow down or speed up for you. Conversely, watch far enough ahead that you can avoid slow merging traffic.

✱ Save your brakes by watching far ahead for stop lights or traffic congestion then begin slowing down by simply letting of in the gas peddle and coasting.

Easy RV Closet Rod Upgrade

I never liked the closet rod in our old fifth wheel. You know, the metal angle iron with the triangular slots for individual clothes hangers. It might work for some RVers… someone thought it was a good idea… but if you want to hang more that few item in the closet, those slots make it nearly impossible.

I lived with it for many years before I finally hung a broomstick from the angle iron as a makeshift closet rod.

When the closet rod broke on our first trip in our new fifth wheel I decided to replace it with a

regular closet rod and do it right this time.

The closet rod and supports were purchased from a local home improvement store. The wood I used to bolster the thin paneling is from a 18″x18″ folding TV table I purchased at Wal-

Mart. The cost of the table was about what it would have cost to buy shelving and it was already finished and was a close match for the RV's cabinets.

I used half the table top for a shelf project and the leftover half I cut in half again to make the two ends for the closet rod. It's a simple project... about an hour... that makes hanging clothes a lot easier.

RV Quick Tips

* Limit your driving time to 5 or 6 hours a day (300 to 350 miles). Some RVers even drive less. Not only will you be more alert, but you will arrive at the campground with plenty of daylight to get set up and settled in before it gets dark. This gives you a chance to unwind, enjoy some of the campground amenities and get rested for another day of travel.

* When passing another vehicle in your RV allow plenty of room and use your turn signals during lane changes. Accelerate until you are well past the other vehicle before pulling back in. Maintain your speed until you are a safe distance ahead of the vehicle you just passed.

* Use a document scanner to scan all your important documents. There are a few that have to be in the original, like a Certificate Of Deposit or a Birth Certificate, but most documents like bank statements, credit card bills and tax returns can be scanned and saved in digital format. By discarding the originals you cut your storage of paper records by 90%.

* Keep a distance of at least 30 feet per 10 mph of speed between you and the vehicle in front of you. 30 feet x 50 MPH = 150 feet.

Replace Hard-to-Reach Waste Valve with a Drain Master

Our Coachmen fifth wheel bunkhouse floor plan was designed with two toilets, one up front and one in the rear. Apparently Coachmen couldn't figure out how or didn't want to spend the extra money to plumb the two together and instead we had to have two sewer hoses going into a 'Y' fitting at the sewer hookup. It was a real hassle and required carrying an extra twenty feet of hose which was difficult to stow.

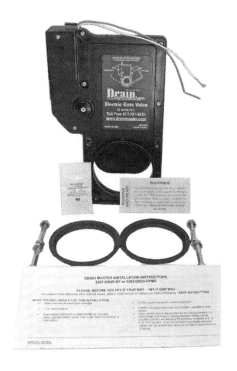

Even worse, to connect a sewer hose or operate the valve on the front holding tank we had to get on hands and knees and crawl under the trailer to reach it! That wouldn't be fun for a young person but for a couple of old folks it was literally a pain. We had to live with it for about six months.

I knew when we bought our new fifth wheel that I would eventually have to do something about the holding tank plumbing. The Drain Master electric waste valve was the key part of the holding tank drain system makeover.

Installing the Drain Master waste valve was the easiest part of the whole project. If you have a hard to reach valve... even if it's not as bad as mine was... you may want to consider replacing it with a Drain Master. If you are just a little handy, you can do it yourself. Phase Four Industries' Drain Master kit has all you need to replace an existing manual valve and the instructions are complete, accurate and easy to follow. No special tools required.

RV Interior Add-ons Make it Home

I like having a place to hang a jacket, my around-the-house jeans, or whatever just needs hanging up. I installed clothes pegs on a bare wall soon after we moved into our first fifth wheel and they were nearly the first things I added to our new fifth wheel.

You can get clothes pegs and hooks of all types, colors and designs so finding some to match the interior of your RV should be possible. I found mine at Home Depot. They are plain but were inexpensive, had reasonably long pegs... important when hanging things like heavy jackets... and had four pegs on one bar... I can never have enough pegs.

The shelf over the door was an add-on too. The space over the door in our new fifth wheel seemed to be the right spot to display my woodcarvings. It took a while but I finally found the shelf at Michaels... a craft store. It was unfinished and was actually too big when I bought it. After, modifying it to fit and spraying it with semi-gloss Deft lacquer it comes acceptably close to matching the cabinetry.

The wood carvings are stuck down with earthquake putty and ride well as-is when traveling.

A word of caution: Be very careful about the length of screw you use. The screws don't need to go into the wall more than a 3/8s inch. Small diameter screws are best. You can also use small plastic anchors and screw into the anchors. But, I have not had a problem so far with just screws.

RV Interior Cosmetic Touch-up Tips

Even the most well-cared-for RVs are sure to show some wear and tear over time. With a little care and ingenuity, many minor defects can be made invisible.

Here are a few products you may already have on hand that can touch up minor scratches, nicks and nail holes on interior woodwork and paneling.

For white surfaces use:

- White-Out, the fluid used to correct spelling errors in typewritten documents. Is this still for sale?

- Acrylic tile caulk

- Plain white toothpaste.

- Acrylic and/or oil artists paints.

- Children's crayons. To match colored surfaces pick a close or matching artist paint or crayon.

- Always try these touch-ups in an inconspicuous area first to make sure.

You may be able to cover large holes, stains or blemishes with a picture, mirror, hanger hooks, or other accessories, depending on where they are located.

Panel seams that have opened up can be covered with a matching trim strip in the same material finish as the wall. Check with your RV tech for after market trim supplies. In some cases you may even be able to find trim that closely matches at a home repair store. It won't look out of place if the trim comes close to the wall paneling.

Upgrade Your RV's Power Cable Hatch

When we first got out new fifth wheel the 30 amp power cord came out of the sidewall through a small round utility hatch. I worried the plug would jiggle back into the storage space behind and I would not be able to reach through the small hole to retrieve it. That didn't happen but what did happen was just as bad.

Hatch Before Upgrade

When storing the cord the day before it somehow got looped over itself so the next day when I tried to hook up again the cord would only come out about six feet. I pushed, pulled and jiggled but couldn't get the loop undone.

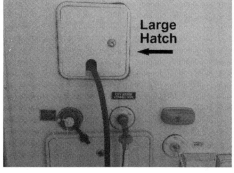

Large Hatch

To get the cord untangled I had to remove the screws and pull the plastic port away from the wall. The actual hole was just large enough that I could reach in and untangle the cord.

After getting the cord loose and pulling it out I looked through the hole at the space behind the wall. It was actually quite large. The wall area was large enough that I could install a larger utility hatch in place of that little round port.

Cutting a large hole in the side of your RV may be just a little intimidating... if you screw it up it would be pretty ugly... but if you are handy with tools and measure carefully I'm confident you can do it.

Thetford Toilet Riser Kit

Like to have the toilet in your RV a little taller? It can be done and without too much effort.

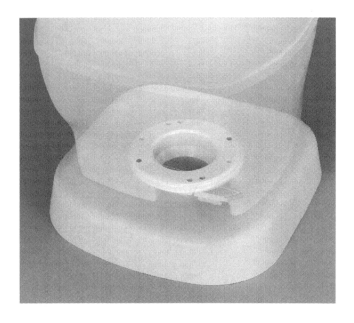

There is a Thetford kit that simplifies things. The kit contains longer bolts, new nuts and two seals in addition to the riser which will lift your toilet 2.5 inches. It is not a difficult job ...not even in the tiny second bathroom in our 5er... I just got my "narrow" son to do it. He definitely fit in the small space better than I would have.

Follow the instructions that come with the kit, but simplified they are:

- Check the water supply line. The toilet will be 2.5" higher and you may have to increase the length of the supply to reach the additional 2.5". Ours did.

- Shut off the water to the RV, drain the toilet and disconnect the supply line. Remove the nuts that secure the toilet to the floor. Lift the toilet up and off the bolts. Clean the base and the flange area and set the toilet aside on newspapers or rags.

- Put the seals in place. Install the long bolts. Position the riser over the bolts. You may need to make a hole in the riser for the waterline.

- Slide toilet down over the bolts and tighten the nuts until the toilet feels secure.

- Check waterline connection once more before turning water back on. With water back on, check for leaks.

- If your toilet has a leaking supply valve or flush valve you should make sure you have the parts on hand to do those repairs while the toilet is already removed.

Toilets installed in newer RVs, especially high end models, are more similar to residential toilets in height so I suppose the use of toilet risers will diminish over time. Still, someone with arthritis or just bad knees will appreciate all the height they can get.

Using Household Furniture in an RV

Using household furniture in your RV will depend on the size and floor plan of the RV you have or intend to buy.

Your first concern will be will it fit through the door? RV Doors are not as wide as house doors and are often flanked by cabinets or walls making it even more difficult to maneuver large furniture through the door. Worst case, you can remove a large window. It's not as big a project as you might think.

Will you have room for it? RVs are designed for efficient use of space so you will probably have to remove something before adding your own furniture.

You will also have to consider how you will secure the furniture when you are traveling. Anything in an RV, especially a motorhome, MUST BE FASTENED DOWN when on the road. If not, the first time you come to a screeching halt, everything loose behind you will head your way at near the speed you were traveling before you stopped.

Weight is going to be an issue as well. One of the reasons RVers want to use household furniture is because it's built better or is larger and more comfortable. Both of these factor into the weight of the furniture.

A fellow RVer wrote, "I tossed the sofa in the RV so I could have a recliner. I also brought in a drop-leaf table that I wanted to use to give me space for sewing and working puzzles, so the swivel rocker in the RV went out the door. I follow the rule — Weight In = Weight Out. Before I buy something I toss out an equal amount of weight."

Travel Trailer Turn Signal & Marker Lights Upgrade

Have you even been pulling your travel trailer or fifth wheel and signaled to make a lane change and the guy next to you just doesn't seem to get the message. You watch your mirror, waiting for him to take some kind of action that will allow you to move over but he just hangs there next to your trailer.

It's bad enough when it happens out on the highway, but when you're in urban traffic trying to maneuver 50 feet of rig for an upcoming turn or lane merge it can get frustrating really fast.

Think about it, if a motorist is just forward of the end of your trailer, there's a good chance he can't see your rear lights and it's possible the turn signal light on your truck is obscured by the front corner of your trailer.

On our old Prowler fifth wheel the back of the truck was very close to the front of the trailer and the truck tail lights were hard to see from the back of the trailer. My solution was to mount a pair of combination signal/ marker lights at the front corner of the fifth wheel.

I really feel the extra signal lights help to make my intention to change lanes apparent to motorists and at night the marker lights help out as well.

When we got our new fifth wheel one of the first modifications I did was to add an extra pair of signal/marker lights the same as those on the old Prowler. And, on the theory that more is better I added two more signal lights to each side. See arrows in photo.

Under RV Sewer Hose Storage Tube

It doesn't take too much RVing experience to learn that, when it comes to hook-ups, every campground and RV park is different.

Most of the time the sewer connection and utilities are reasonably close and convenient but then there are times when you have to get out the RV extension cord, an extra 25' of water hose and another 20' of sewer hose.

Now storing an RV extension cord and extra water hose isn't a big deal but finding space for an extra 20 feet of stinky sewer hose can be a problem. You can only stuff one hose in the bumper. What do you do with the other one?

For the longest time I've been storing mine in a plastic tote box I keep in the truck bed. It works but it's less than ideal.

Every since we got our new fifth wheel I've wanted to make one of those storage tubes that hang under the RV. I'm sure you've seen several types of commercial storage tubes but they are not in my budget.

Anyway, I've put off the project mostly because I couldn't work out in my head a parts list and plan of action. Looking at all the different commercial types just confused the issue. I have planned to head for the big orange home improvement store and do a little brainstorming but just haven't made the time.

Well, now I don't have the excuse of not having a parts list and plan of action thanks to a member of the RVbasics Yahoo Group. She provided the group with a parts list and basic instructions.

http://rvbasics.com/techtips/RV-Sewer-Hose-Storage.html instructions she and her husband used to make theirs. You can find them on the RV Basics website.
http://rvbasics.com/techtips/RV-Sewer-Hose-Storage.html

Give Your Truck Box Some Space

Do you have a truck box in the bed of your pickup? Consider setting it 5 to 6 inches back from the front wall of the bed. I got the idea many years ago and it worked out so well I made the space just a little bigger when we got our current pickup. The space made between the truck box and the wall makes a great place to store leveling boards and blocks. In the same space I also store the sections of rain gutter I use to support my sewer hose.

Having that special storage area minimized the clutter in the truck bed and keeps the boards and blocks easy to reach.

There are a couple negatives to setting the box back:

- Leaves, pine needles etc. have to be cleaned out of the space occasionally and that can be a hassle.

- Depending on how far you set the storage box back and how wide it is, the box can block the view of a fifth wheel hitch. My old truck box wasn't as wide and I could see the hitch, in my current truck I can't. It's not a problem for me, I learned how to hitch up backing my Dad's big rig under a semi-trailer... couldn't see the hitch or the kingpin.

If you can't see your hitch you can make a small marker at the center of the length of the truck box as a guide to line up the kingpin since the hitch is centered in the truck bed.

A Reflection on RV Safety

I'm not obsessed with safety but I try to keep safe and if $18 and a little time will make my rig a little more visible at night I'm up for it.

I purchased a couple packages of reflective decals at Wal-Mart the last time we were there and applied them to my fifth wheel and truck.

I also put two strips of red reflectors just below the tailgate at the back of the truck but forgot to ask Fran to take a photo.

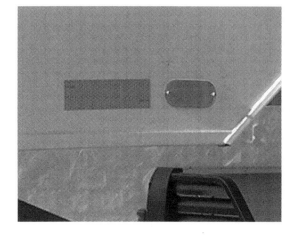

Miscellaneous RV Tips

Carbon Monoxide Detector Operation and Safety Tips

Modern RVs come equipped with a carbon monoxide detector to detect unsafe levels of carbon monoxide. If the alarm sounds take the following steps:

- If you are driving, open all the windows until the driver can come to a safe place to stop.

- Once you are able to stop, shut off the engine, and the generator if running, and exit the vehicle.

- Allow the vehicle to ventilate, then search for the source of the carbon monoxide, such as generator exhaust.

- Do not re-enter the vehicle until you have determined that it is safe to do so.

- When running the generator, it is best to keep the windows nearest to the generator exhaust closed, to prevent excess carbon monoxide from entering the cabin.

Like the smoke detector, the carbon monoxide detector will "chirp" when the 9-volt battery is low.

When you need to replace the battery, follow these steps:

- Remove the alarm by twisting the case in a counter-clockwise motion.

- Remove and discard the used battery.

- Install the new battery.

- Check to make sure that the battery is seated properly. You can test the alarm while it is off the mounting bracket by pushing the test button

- Reinstall the alarm by twisting the case in a clockwise motion.

- Retest the alarm.

Check Book Checkup

You may think you have taken precautions to maintain good control of your checkbook and credit cards but a stealthy thief or quick robber can snatch something from you when you least expect it. These tips may help you prevent that from happening or at least render your property useless to the crook.

- Have your checks printed with your first initial and middle initial and your last name. Make sure your bank knows you will always use your full first and last name when signing your checks. If a thief uses just your initials they will know it is not you making out the check.

- Consider a Post Office Box or a Personal Mail Box for a place to receive your mail. Without your residence address on your checks a thief that obtains your checkbook cannot find your home. An added benefit of a Personal Mail Box is somewhere your mail can be held and forwarded when you are on the road.

- Don't have phone numbers, Social Security numbers or other such personal information printed on your checks. If a business needs them for identification they can ask. You will know who you gave them to and other merchants don't need them.

- When you get a new credit card, don't sign your name on the back, Write: Photo Identification Required or Photo ID Required. I have never understood why they say to sign them. Once a thief has your card and your signature he's set to go!

- There are not many businesses that require checks instead of Debit or Credit cards these days so your checkbook might be safer at home with your other important papers.

Coffee filters Have Many Uses in an RV

After all the years we have lived and traveled together, Steven knew I didn't have a coffee maker that required filters, so of course he asked about the filters as I unpacked grocery bags one day.

"I've seen many suggestions for alternate uses of these filters and I decided to try a few before passing them along as tips," I told him.

Coffee filters are lint free and very light… great for many uses in an RV. I got my supply of filters, the kind with the flat bottoms and two and a quarter inch sides, for 99 cents (plus tax, of course). Here are some handy tips for using them.

- First thing I tried, as I sat contemplating, was to clean my glasses. Perfect size and did a great job of it.

- I use the mirror in my bathroom to make notes with a dry erase pen. The filter cleaned off the old notes quickly and efficiently.

- Folded in half, and half again, the triangle that is formed can be used to gently clean the dust from a computer screen.

- The filters make great covers for dishes when cooking or reheating in a microwave.

- Cork pieces in your wine bottle? Pour the wine through a coffee filter to remove the cork chunks.

- A filter in the bottom of a pot you are planting will permit water to drain while it keeps the soil from exiting.

- Poke the stick of a popsicle through a filter or put one around the stick and fluff it out a bit to catch drippings and keep your kid or grandkid sticky-free.

- When putting away a cast iron skillet put a filter in it to prevent rust by absorbing any remaining moisture.

- Line a sieve or strainer with a coffee filter and pour frying oil through it for recycling.

- Use a handy coffee filter on your kitchen scale when weighing chopped foods.

- A great dauber for razor nicks. Stash a few in the bathroom.

- Use several for thicker absorbing on a plate beneath bacon or fries to soak up the grease.

- A filter makes a good holder for tacos, burritos, juicy sandwiches or wraps.

- A couple filters between stacked dishes and cups will protect your china on the road.

- Share popcorn with the whole family in filter bowls for everyone.

- Make a spice or herb pouch with a filter with a tied top for soup or stew flavoring.

- Put garlic cloves in a filter and twist the top. Heat it in the microwave for 10 or 15 seconds to make them peel easier when skins split.

- A coffee filter bundled around fresh bay leaves and tied up to make little pouches can be placed on pantry shelves to drive away bugs. They don't tolerate the smell of the leaves.

- Place a filter over the flash on a camera to diffuse the harsh light on a baby's eyes.

- Use a filter as a good throw-away applicator for shoe polish, silver polish, filler for scratches or scrapes on furniture.

- Give toddlers treats …cookies, crackers, dry cereal, raisins, M & Ms, etc. …in a coffee filter that is easier to hold onto with tiny hands.

Common Myths Dispelled

As the weather begins to warm around the country, drivers begin thinking of spring and the services needed to maintain their vehicles. Unfortunately, it's during this time of year, that automotive myths are often unintentionally perpetuated.

Knowing which stories are myths and which ones are fact can be difficult. Because of that, NAPA AutoCare's 2009 Technician of the Year, Jack Gregory, is dispelling some common myths to keep everyone's vehicle running smoothly in 2009.

Myth: Filling your cooling system with all water and no anti-freeze will save you money while not harming your vehicle.

Fact: The vehicle's cooling system requires a mixture of half water, half anti-freeze. "Too much anti-freeze causes the vehicle to run on higher than optimal temperatures," cautions Gregory. "Too much water can cause lower operating temperatures and possible freezing."

Myth: Driving at 56 mph will give you the best fuel economy.

Fact: Although most vehicle manufacturers base their product's gas mileage at 56 mph, driving at that speed doesn't guarantee the best gas mileage. Keeping a consistent speed, whether it's 25 mph or 65 mph, will ensure the best fuel economy.

Myth: Over inflating tires helps with gas mileage.

Fact: Over inflated tires cause wear in the middle of the tire. Under inflated tires causes wear on the outside of the tire. Drivers should inflate tires to the car maker's recommended pressure to maintain maximum fuel economy and improve the life of the tires.

Myth: Driving closely behind an 18-wheeler will protect you from headwinds and allow your car to use less gas.

Fact: Driving closely behind an 18-wheeler doesn't help with gas mileage, is dangerous and can be illegal. A sudden stop from the 18-wheeler could force a driver to slam on the brakes or even worse, cause an accident.

Myth: A vehicle can run a long way with the fuel gauge on empty.

Fact: Once a gas gauge reaches empty, about two gallons of gasoline remain in the vehicle's tank. It's always best to not test your vehicle's limits, especially with colder weather affecting most of the country.

Fifth Wheel RV Stabilizing

To optimize the stability of your fifth wheel trailer you need to have a fair amount of weight on the rear jacks. But it's nearly impossible get much weight on them using the hand crank without breaking your back.

The easiest way I've found to save my back is to get the trailer nearly level, but just a little lower toward the front. I crank down the rear leveling jacks good and snug but without straining my back.

Once the rear jacks are down and snug, I raise the front of the fifth wheel to level using the the landing gear. The procedure works very well, you just need to be careful not to put too much weight on the rear jacks. Be conservative the first few times you do it until you have a good idea of the amount of weight you are transferring to the jacks.

Using the above procedure along with a wheel chock between the wheels (the type that 'clamps' the tires) and a king pin jack I manage to create a very stable home.

Save Your RVing Memories

Seeing new sights is a big part of what makes RVing so great. Of course we all like to take photos of the places we've been, not only to show family and friends back home but as reminders to us.

This Tip is offered by RVer Richard Bauer:

Like many of you we use a digital camera to record photos of our travels. A couple of days ago while touring the Bandeleir National Monument in New Mexico I discovered that 100+ photos that I had taken at the monument and at another location during the previous day had vanished. They were no longer on the memory card. A few minutes later (after taking a few more photos) it happened again. The memory card was self-erasing itself.

I normally download the photos from the camera to our laptop every day but I neglected to do that the night before. As a result of my inattention we lost a lot of photos. It could have been worse. I could have lost a whole weeks worth as the memory card can store 365 very high-res images. I should've known better.

I am a fanatic about backing up the data, programs and operating system files on our computers. In fact I maintain multiple copies of each backup on separate hard drives. For whatever reason I just never thought of our camera as a computer but that's exactly what it is and I should have been treating it accordingly.

Had I done the download the night before it wouldn't have prevented the loss of the photos of the Bandeleir NM, but maybe I wouldn't have lost the photos from the day before.

The moral of the story and consider this the 'tip': learn from my mistake and download the photos from your camera to your hard drive(s) frequently… daily is best… and then be sure to backup those files. You never can tell when your digital camera will malfunction.

The Myth About Diesel Engine Idling

Some diesel engine owners think it's good, even necessary, to let their engines idle for twenty or thirty minutes after startup or before shut down. Truth is, besides being wearisome to neighbors excessive idling can be harmful to your engine.

If running hard or pulling up hill, the engine may need to be run as long as 5 minutes at idle to uniformly cool internal components and reject heat away from turbo bearings; running slowly off the Interstate ramp and driving at low power levels to the fuel stop or campground counts toward the idling time before shutting down.

Engine Manufactures do NOT recommend excessive idling of the engines, since it can cause excessive carbon buildup on the pistons, piston rings, injector tips, valves, etc.

Transmission Torque Converter Not Staying Locked?

This tip came from something I read. The RVer had a pickup tow vehicle and complained that the torque converter would not stay locked. He said the converter would just unlock seemingly with no reason then almost immediately lock up again. It happened both in overdrive and out of overdrive. There was more to his description but I can't remember. The suggested solution from the RV tech follows.

Have a problem with the torque converter on your motorhome or tow vehicle not staying locked up? Check for a faulty brake light switch or throttle position sensor.

Any time you tap the brakes, the brake light switch sends a signal to unlock the converter, so if it's faulty your torque converter will act up.

A faulty throttle position sensor may be the cause of your problem especially if the symptoms seem to be heat sensitive since it is positioned where heat builds up that can damage the sensor and or wires.

Trailer Wiring Converter for Imported Tow Vehicles

Imported and some domestic tow vehicles use international lighting in which the turn signal lights are wired separate from the brake lights. Generally an amber lens is used for turn signal lights while standard red lens are used for stop lights.

The lighting system for most American made vehicles combines the turn signals and brake lights into one wire instead of two, and has no amber lenses.

If the tow vehicle has an international system, the two separate wires for turn signals and brake lights on the tow vehicle must be combined into one for the travel trailer's lighting system to work properly. To do this, a converter is necessary.

The converter is a circuit board built into a separate weather proof box or built into a tow vehicle plug connector.

Three or four wires coming from the tow vehicle… left and right turn, and brake wires… go into the converter and two come out. The two wires coming out are connected to the left and right turn connectors in the trailer-plug receptacle.

Get the Most From RV Air Conditioners

- Here are a few tips to save energy and make your RV air conditioner work as efficiently as possible.

- Keep the shades or blinds in the RV closed to help your AC perform faster and better.

- If possible, close doors to areas of your RV not used.

- Park in the shade to keep your RV as cool as possible.

RV Quick Tips

✱ Always keep cash handy for paying the tolls on toll roads, bridges, tunnels, and ferries.

✱ When you've parked your RV in a new campsite and you're hooking up your water hose, hook it up to the spigot first and run a fair amount of water through. This does several things, 1, it flushes your water hose, 2, lets you see what the water is like… could be rusty or dirty or smelly, 3, fills the hose with water which eliminates most of the sputtering at the RV's sink faucets.

Instead of wasting it, water a nearby tree or the grass. If you're parked in a 'parking lot' site and you don't want to make a mess run the water into the sewer.

✱ While on the road, whenever you stop for any kind of break, take time to check your rig. Do a visual inspection and be sure you check the hitch, electrical umbilical, awning and especially the tires and wheels.

✱ An air conditioner not only lowers the temperature of the air but also conditions the air by removing moisture and filtering it. Because moisture is involved, humidity is a large factor in how efficient your air conditioner will operate.

Secure RV Doors and Drawers For Travel Like a Flight Attendant

RVer Darlene Durham offers this tip:

I begin by turning on a light in each area of our motorhome, which for us is the bedroom, bathroom and kitchen/living area. I start in the furthest corner of the bedroom and push on each overhead cabinet door and every drawer to ensure it is latched. Sometimes a cabinet door or drawer looks closed but it may not be latched and can fly open during the movement of travel. I also ensure the closet doors and the door to the bathroom are secure as I make my way around the room. When all is secure in the bedroom, I turn off the light as I move to the bathroom and repeat the process in each room until I get to the front of the motorhome.

If I am interrupted during the process, I look to see which room's light is still on. If the light is off, I know I finished that room. If the light is on, I know I did not complete securing that room and will start over from the beginning in that room. I always double check that I secured our mirrored closet doors and glass shower door as a glass door banging open during travel could result in broken glass.

The contents inside the cabinets and drawers also need to be secured such as putting non-slip material between dishes and packing contents, including refrigerator contents, tightly to avoid movement. When first starting out RVing, we recommend you have a checklist for securing all areas of your RV for travel until you get a process in place that works for you. This "flight attendant" process only takes a few minutes and has worked well for us for years in ensuring all doors and drawers are latched and secure for travel.

A note from Darlene Durham: As long time RVers with tens of thousands of miles traveling in our RVs, we like to think we have learned a thing or two about RVs and the RV lifestyle. We hope you will join us on the road and enjoy this wonderful way of traveling. Get more tips about RVs and RVing at our website http://www.lovetorv.com.

Beware of the Gypsies!

Gypsies. They're out there seeking victims. There are thousands of criminal "families" that practice all the con games known to man. These are the same people that do roofing, driveway surfacing and too many more scams to list. Their activities have been described in books, on TV, in many magazine and newspaper articles.

They also victimize RV buyers. The gypsies buy sub-standard, off brand, RVs direct from factories and peddle them. No dealer will ever honor the warranty papers from these manufacturers.

You will sometimes find them in RV parks, often towing the trailer with a 'work' truck used in their other scams. The trailer will usually be nearly new but not a well-known brand and have a 'for sale' sign on it.

They will be charming as con artists usually are and they'll have wives and children, who are part of the con. They will always have a good story to tell you about why they are desperate to sell. BE CAREFUL!

RV Quick Tips

✱   When several vehicles collect behind your RV, pull off the road at a safe place to let the cars go by. Not only is this common courtesy it is also the law in many states.

✱   When the temperature drops, driving conditions change. Wet roads become icy and dangerous black ice is difficult to see.

RVing With Pets

Tips for RVing With Dogs

by Contributors: Jack and Julee Meltzer

1. In the U.S. alone each year, more than 30 million people take their pets with them on RV trips. While there are numerous issues to consider while RVing with dogs, the tips below are some of the most important.

2. Make Sure that Your Dog Can't Get Lost. Either train your dog to come when called or make absolutely sure that they're on a leash at all times.

3. Get All Vaccinations Up to Date. If your dog gets into an altercation with another animal (or a person), the central issue will become their rabies shots. If you stay at a campground that has a demanding pet policy, you'll need to verify your dog's vaccination records. If you cross into Canada, you'll have to confirm that your dog has had its shots.

4. Make Your Dog Easy to Identify. If your dog does get lost, the ability to easily identify it will become critical. For permanent identification purposes, consider tattoos or microchips. At a minimum, make sure the dog wears tags that show its name, the

date of the last rabies vaccination and your current phone number.

5. Clean Up After Your Dog. The biggest complaint other RVers have about dogs has nothing to do with their bark, their bite, or their behavior.

6. Learn How to Provide First Aid to Your Dog. Although there are ways to get help while on the road, it always takes more time. In the meantime, your ability to provide competent first aid could save your dog's life.

7. Involve Your Dog in Your Activities. If you really want your dogs to have a good time, include them in everything you do.

8. Call the Campgrounds Before You Go. Even if a park claims they're pet-friendly, always call ahead to confirm their policy regarding your dog. "Pet-friendly" may mean dogs weighing under 20 pounds and there may be other restrictions.

9. Plan Ahead for the Unexpected. Have a plan (for your dogs) in case of a flat tire, a serious accident, or a fire in your RV. Start with a few extra leashes and a pet carrier.

10. Learn About Your Camping Environment. The U.S. is a huge country with a vast assortment of dangerous wildlife and treacherous plants, you might inadvertently be putting your dog, and yourself, in danger.

11. Recognize and Respect the Views of Others. While some of us can't imagine traveling without dogs, others can't image traveling with them. If you keep your dog under control and clean up after him, you won't give others anything to grumble about.

RV Quick Tips

✱ To keep the soap from sliding off the shelf in the shower clean the shelf of all soap residue and dry thoroughly. Then apply several small dabs of silicon caulk to the front edge of the shelf. You don't want a continuos bead because water needs to have a way to drain off the shelf.

✱ Our fifth wheel has two entry doors with separate keys. To tell the difference I just removed the plastic cap from the rear door key. The plastic cap on the front door key... the one we use most... makes it easier to find on my key ring. The rear door key is on the same ring next to the front door key so it's easy to find too.

Your Four-Legged RVing & Workout Buddy

Just as it would be hard for you to go out and jog for 45 minutes if you haven't worked out in 6 months, it's also hard for your dog if it is not used to a regular exercise period. Be sure to get your veterinarian's okay before beginning your pet's exercise routine. Pat Robbins from the RVPets forum offers these tips to help you get started:

- Start slowly, gradually increasing the time and intensity of the activity. This will safely strengthen your dog's muscles, aerobic capacity, and footpads.

- Pay attention to how your dog is feeling. Signs that your pet needs to slow down or stop include drooling, stumbling, trouble breathing, and a long, droopy tongue. Take a break and consider making tomorrow's workout shorter. Also remember that in hot weather your dog can't sweat like you do to keep cool.

- Concrete and asphalt [and different sized gravel, pebbles and stones found in many RV parks] are tough on your friends' paws–especially on hot days. Try to walk or run on dirt paths (or grass) as much as possible.

- The longer you work out, the more water Fido needs. Bring along a collapsible water dish to help your pet stay hydrated.

- Be realistic about your pet's limitations. Many smaller breeds love going for a brisk walk, but you'll probably have to carry them on a strenuous hike. Animals with a thin coat will not tolerate cold weather very well, whereas dogs with thick coats don't do well in the summer heat.

- You should avoid strenuous exercise with your dog until he is finished growing (after 9-12 months for most dogs).

RVing With Your Pet

Pets are a big part of people's lives and RVers are no exception. There are many pets of various kinds that travel to all parts of the country to be with their owners. For those of you who cannot imagine traveling without your pets here are a few tips for RV life on the road with your feathered or furry friends.

Pre-trip your pet's paperwork:

Update vaccinations

- Gather up medical records, rabies certificate, license and insurance papers if you have him insured, medications and prescriptions.

- Make sure you have a color photograph of your pet to take along.

Your pet's personal paraphernalia (as needed for type of pet):

- Collar and tags

- At least two leashes

- Grooming equipment

- First aid supplies ... include flea and tick repellent

- Travel crate/cage

- Bedding material

- Favorite toys

- Necessities:

- Food and water bowls/containers

- Ample food that pet is used to

- Pooper scooper bags

- Extra towels and cleaner for mishaps or bad weather

- Special treats

Information:

- When making reservations at a campground, park or resort be sure they permit pets.

- When arriving ask about pet areas, and the location of veterinary services if your pet has health issues.

- Read the park's pet rules and follow them.

- There are always some strange people that do not like pets, but you need to respect their rights anyway.

RV Quick Tips

✳ When storing your RV don't forget the refrigerator/ freezer. After removing all food items, wash the interior walls, shelves and door liner with a solution of 2 tablespoons of baking soda and 1 quart warm water, and wipe dry. Leave the doors open while the RV is in storage.

✳ Faulty batteries cause more car starting problems than any other factor. At 0 degrees, a battery has 35 percent less starting power than in summer. At minus 20, battery power drops 50 percent.

✳ If your battery is more than three years old, have a load test performed by a mechanic.

✳ To avoid frozen door locks, buy a lubricant available in most auto supply stores. If your lock freezes, heat your key with a pocket lighter but remember to wear gloves or hold the key with pliers.

Thank You!

Thank you for purchasing our Best RV Tips book. Your purchase helps to keep us on the road so we truly appreciate your support.

We Need Your Book Review

If you found reading this compilation of RV tips enjoyable and the tips helpful, a book review by you would be greatly appreciated. Good or bad every review is very important. We always need new, current reviews. Your review will let new buyers know our book remains timely and relevant. Please take a few minutes now to visit the book's sales page and leave a review. You can find the link to the sales page at: **http://RVTipOfTheDay.com/links**

Get Connected With Fellow RVers

No single book could cover all the RV tips that exist so we set up the RVTips email discussion group on Yahoo Groups to allow members to share their RVing tips, experiences and knowledge with fellow RVers. To join the group, visit the group's home page.

http://autos.groups.yahoo.com/group/RVTips

If you would prefer a web forum instead of an email group we have one for you. You can join the RVTipOfTheDay forum at http://rvtipoftheday.com/forum

If you are a Facebook user, you can follow us and join in at:

http://www.facebook.com/RVTipOfTheDay

Can't decide which is best for you? Why not join all three. They are free and you can unsubscribe anytime.

Lastly, you are invited to visit our companion website RVBasics.com http://RVBasics.com You will find hundreds of RV articles there.

Remember: You can find up-to-date Clickable links to all web links in your book at: http://RVTipOfTheDay.com/links

87420237R00117

Made in the USA
Columbia, SC
13 January 2018